IVA, BANKRUPTCY AND OTHER DEBT SOLUTIONS

The Definitive Guide

IVA, Bankruptcy and other Debt Solutions

The Definitive Guide

By

James Falla

Blue Sky Publishing
London

First published in the United Kingdom in 2006 by:
Blue Sky Books, an imprint of
Thomas Charles & Co Ltd
164, Acton High Street
London
W3 6QZ

ISBN: 0-9553504-0-9
978-0-9553504-0-5

Thanks go to both William Berry & Jake Wallis Simons
for their significant contribution and without whom, this
book would not have been possible

Cover design: Simone Poggiali (net121.com)

Contents

For more debt help and resources as well as a support forum, please visit the official site for this book: www.iva-book.com

Preface

If your debts are driving you mad, you're not alone. For millions of people across the UK, debt is a serious problem. The Debt Advisory Company, Thomas Charles & Co Ltd, recently commissioned a YouGov survey which showed that:

- Around 3.8 million adults in the UK have unsecured debts totalling £20,000 or more;

- Around 8 million have unsecured debts of £10,000 or more;

- more than 1 million of these are 'quite likely', 'very likely' or 'certain' to declare themselves insolvent.

Clearly, debt in the UK is a very big problem indeed.

As anyone with serious debt will testify, the stress that it can cause is tremendous, and its impact on everyday quality of life can be severe. Peace of mind is destroyed, work performances decline, relationships suffer and even health can be affected. To make matters worse, every month the financial mess gets more complicated and confusing.

As you will see from the 'case file' sections throughout this book, many people have found that a single event triggers their debt problem. This event may be a redundancy, an income gap, a one-off expense such as a wedding, a period of bad money-management or simply a stroke of bad luck. Whatever the reason, debts start to mount. Repayments may seem manageable at first, but due to an unaffordable lifestyle or sudden expenses, they can soon snowball out of control. Gradually, what was originally a useful credit facility can turn into a heavy burden. Eventually, as the banks and credit companies turn up the pressure, people feel forced to rob Peter to pay Paul – borrowing money from one creditor and offering it to another.

At this point it is important to acknowledge that the problem is becoming a crisis. Monthly payments may be sustained, but this is causing the total debt to mount, which is making matters worse, not better. If nothing is done to remedy the situation, sooner or later credit facilities will dry up. Payments will be missed, default notices will be issued, and eventually the creditors may file for bankruptcy. If their argument is fair, little can be done to avoid it; even if the debtor refuses to comply with bankruptcy proceedings, a Bankruptcy Order can still be made. Therefore, if you are finding yourself robbing Peter to pay Paul, the time to act is now. In my experience, many people naturally react by burying their head in the sand and trying to 'struggle on,' but this is absolutely the worst thing to do. It is far better to take action to resolve the debt once and for all, which means getting the right advice about the debt solutions discussed in this book.

In 1998, when I first started working with people in serious debt, the debt problem in the UK was big. Now it is huge, and growing all the time. We are currently facing a situation where the total amount of UK debt is larger than the Gross National Income. This is a frightening fact by anyone's standards; but it also means that solutions do exist, and people are finding ways out of debt all the time. Whatever your difficulties are, there are tried-and-tested ways of sorting them out. In 2004 I set up my own Debt Advisory Company, Thomas Charles & Co Ltd, to help people in serious debt benefit from these solutions. Since that time thousands of our clients have put their money worries behind them for good. On a personal level, it is extremely rewarding to know that Thomas Charles & Co Ltd has helped so many people solve their debt problems. Now, with the help of this book, you can do the same.

Kind Regards,

James Falla

Director, Thomas Charles & Co Ltd

Introduction

Are we playing the system – or is the system playing us?

We live in strange times. Over the last ten years, our standard of living and expectations of life have increased massively. Back in the early 90's, people were satisfied with a single car, one holiday a year, and a couple of visits to a restaurant per month; these days, it is absolutely normal to own two cars, go on two holidays a year, and to eat out in a restaurant once or twice a week. Moreover, our emphasis on convenience means that even simple needs have become more expensive. Cooking a meal at home, for example, is less about buying an onion and half a pound of mince, and more about purchasing expensive ready-meals and packaged foodstuffs. These days, for every labour-intensive activity there is an expensive shortcut. And as a society we are becoming so used to paying for these shortcuts that we are beginning to forget that there was ever another way of doing things. We are developing a more and more intense craving for instant gratification, which fosters a ubiquitous buy-now-pay-later attitude. Our culture is one of convenience, of consumerism; gone are the days when people would save up over an extended period in order to purchase the things they want.

All too often, wages do not rise at the same rate as our spending patterns; as a result, we live in a climate where borrowing is absolutely acceptable and normal. We are more willing to borrow, and in parallel to this, banks are more willing to lend. Our instant-fix culture goes hand-in-hand with getting into debt – the banks' attitude towards lending mirrors our attitude towards borrowing. Banks are strongly motivated to sell credit, and have increasingly fewer scruples as to who they sell to. They offer extortionate Payment

Protection, and often charge high levels of interest. Most 17-year-olds will be bombarded with credit card offers before they turn 18, and even those with bad credit ratings are being targeted by lenders. As a society, we are evolving towards a situation where debt is the lifeblood of our economy.

The result of this dog-eat-dog melee is that we end up playing the system, and the system ends up playing us. When we go to a bank for credit, or consider buying something on finance, we are met with sales people who are bonused on selling credit. It is almost impossible these days to receive good, objective advice, especially in banks and building societies. Lending money is big business, and the staff who advise us are absolutely incentivised to sell us as much credit as possible. Of course, due to stringent regulations they cannot engage in direct deception; to be fair to them, all the facts are usually on the table before we sign on the dotted line. However, the sales staff – being sales staff – present the idea of borrowing in a way that might not be altogether in the interests of the consumer. They do everything they can to make sure that the consequences of borrowing are not foremost in your mind. They place little emphasis on the length of the payback period, and aim to draw your attention away from the fact that you will be paying back a significant amount of interest over a prolonged period of time. On occasion, they are even prone to hitting below the belt. This happened to me recently, when I bought some furniture from a High Street supplier. When it was time to sign the finance agreement, the sales person simply pointed to the box and I signed it. Imagine how flabbergasted I was when several days later it emerged that the box he had pointed to – and I had signed – stated 'Payment Protection required'! (I would be the *last* person to sign up for Payment Protection; the reasons for this are explored in Chapter 4). Luckily I managed to get the agreement revoked, but this example illustrates the techniques that sales people often employ when attempting to sell you credit and Payment Protection.

In response to this, more and more people are learning to play the system. Information about debt solutions is far more readily available these days, particularly on the Internet, and people are becoming more aware that the consequences of serious debt may not be as bad as they once thought. Our increased familiarity with debt solutions is beginning to influence our decision to borrow. This is especially the case in areas such as the South East, where millions of people are finding it impossible to get on the property ladder. Fewer people own a home, and are therefore able to borrow money with relative impunity – this is especially true amongst young people and graduates. The recent YouGov survey commissioned by Thomas Charles & Co Ltd indicated that 28% of those living in rented accommodation and 16% of those in the 25–34 age group are at risk of personal insolvency in the UK. It appears that if you don't own a property, you don't have so much to lose, and when this fact becomes widely acknowledged it encourages people – particularly young people – to borrow irresponsibly. The solutions described in this book, such as bankruptcy and IVA, do bring with them a certain amount of discomfort and lifestyle restriction; but people are beginning to feel that it might be worth it.

I would wholeheartedly advise against any attempt to play the system. In reality, proposing IVAs and declaring bankruptcy are anything but soft options. They do have far-reaching financial effects, and must be treated very seriously. I would strongly suggest that you research the four different debt solutions using this book, obtain professional advice, and support your chosen solution with good money management by following the four basic points explained in Chapter 5.

What solutions are available?

In this book, you will find a comprehensive explanation of the four main debt solutions available in England, Ireland and Wales (Scottish law is beyond the scope of this book). These are:

- Individual Voluntary Arrangement (IVA)

- Bankruptcy

- Debt Management Plan

- Debt Consolidation

The first two solutions involve legal agreements between you and your creditors, whereby the creditors often write off a significant portion of the total debt. The second two are 'informal solutions', which mean that no legal process is involved and the creditors still demand the full amount to be repaid.

The chapters that follow will explain these four solutions one by one in a straightforward, easy-to-understand way. Which solution will work for you depends on a variety of factors including the amount of money you owe, whether you are a homeowner or a tenant, how much money you earn, what you do for a living and so on; each chapter deals with these issues point-by-point, giving a list of key questions and answers. At the end of each chapter will be a section called 'What To Do Next', providing all the information you need to set the ball rolling.

Whichever of the four solutions you choose, you will almost certainly benefit from improving your budgeting skills and money-management. Time and time again I have seen people attempt to put a debt solution in place, only to make the situation worse a few months later due to a financially inefficient lifestyle. That is, even though the debt solution is adequate, they fail to remedy their bad money-management and excessive spending habits – often the very reason they are in debt in the first place! To help over-come these obstacles, Chapter 5, 'Managing your money', explains simple, reliable techniques for organising your finances and keeping your bills affordable. Finally, the Appendix at the back of the book features a budget-sheet and creditor-list that you can use to keep track of your personal finances – often the simplest methods are the best!

Whatever solution you eventually find for your debt problems, I hope that this book helps you to see some light at the end of the tunnel, leaving you debt-free and able to turn over a new leaf. In this way you will join the thousands of other satisfied Thomas Charles & Co Ltd clients who now enjoy lasting financial security.

Chapter One

Individual Voluntary Arrangement: IVA

The IVA is generally seen as an option for those who wish to avoid bankruptcy. Whereas bankruptcy has been around since 1571, the IVA was introduced in the Insolvency Act of 1986. At the time there was no legal alternative to bankruptcy, and under the bankruptcy laws the creditors were suffering huge financial losses. The IVA was introduced to allow creditors to receive more money back than bankruptcy would offer. In order to facilitate this, an IVA places no employment restrictions on the debtor, so that there is nothing preventing them from paying back as much as they can manage. Furthermore, an IVA allows the debtor to keep their house on condition they release as much equity as they can towards the debt; this means that the creditors receive the equity more easily than they would if the house were to be seized and sold through bankruptcy proceedings. Of course, the IVA has significant advantages for the debtor as well. The main benefit is that the creditors will write off any outstanding debt once the debtor has fulfilled their side of the deal. Thus it allows responsible debtors to avoid bankruptcy by coming to a win-win arrangement with their creditors.

What is an IVA?

An IVA is a legal contract between you and your creditors. It enables you to cut your debts to an affordable level and settle them over a fixed period. An IVA ensures that you retain control of your home and under most circumstances your job is not at risk. What's more, it is a totally private arrangement – nobody needs to know about it apart from you, your advisors and your creditors. Most importantly of all, the IVA allows you to settle your debts by paying as much as you can realistically afford to your creditors within a fixed period. That is, an IVA means you are not running away from the problem, but making every effort to put things right.

As the IVA is a legal agreement, you cannot propose one by yourself. The person who would be in charge of proposing and overseeing your IVA is called an Insolvency Practitioner (best described as a specialist solicitor). Your first point of contact, however, would usually be a Debt Advisor. A Debt Advisor would discuss your situation with you, and advise as to whether or not an IVA would work. If you decide to proceed with the IVA, the Debt Advisor would complete a draft proposal that would be passed to the Insolvency Practitioner to finalise. From then on, the matter would be between you and the Insolvency Practitioner.

Essentially, within an IVA you would propose to make one single manageable monthly payment, based on your budget, for up to 5 years. If you are a homeowner and there is equity in your house, you would also offer to release some of this as part of the Arrangement. Once the agreement has been honoured, the remaining debt is wiped clean, leaving you completely debt-free. This means that an IVA can write off up to 75% of your debts! This all might sound too good to be true, and in many ways it is very good indeed. However, under the terms of the agreement you undertake to contribute as much as possible within your budget. So in reality, an IVA presents an opportunity for you to pay as you can in a manageable way – a way you can afford.

IVA: the advantages

- You can fulfil your sense of duty by paying pack as much as you can, while still having enough to live on.

- Your creditors undertake to write off debt which cannot be reasonably repaid. This could be up to 75% of your debt.

- All further interest and charges are frozen.

- Student Loan Company debts may be included within the IVA, and part of it consequently written off.

- You retain control of your house (although you may have to release available equity).

- Your reasonable assets will not be put at risk.

- You would not be subject to any employment restrictions, unless specifically prescribed in your contract of employment.

- The whole process is totally private and discreet.

IVA: the disadvantages

- Under the terms of the IVA, you may be locked into a payment plan for up to 5 years.

- If you are a homeowner, you will have to release available equity from the property.

- If you fail to make your IVA contributions without a good reason, or if you do not meet the requirements of the IVA, you run the risk of being made bankrupt.

- While in an IVA, you cannot take significant unsecured credit. Additionally, the IVA would affect your credit rating for 6 years, meaning that any mortgage you take during this time would incur higher interest rates. You may also need to put down a larger deposit than is usually required.

Questions and Answers

Q　How do I know if I qualify for an IVA?

A　To qualify for an IVA, your debt normally needs to be at least £15000–£20000 (there is no upper limit). This figure should be inclusive of all interest and charges; 'settlement figures' are not appropriate when proposing an IVA. You might like to use the creditor-sheet in the Appendix at the back of the book to keep track of all your creditors and work out exactly how much you owe in total.

In addition to this, you need to be able to afford the monthly IVA payments. The amount of your monthly payments will depend on two things: how much you owe, and how much you can afford. To find out the exact figure, consult a professional Debt Advisor such as those at Thomas Charles & Co Ltd. As a rule of thumb, however, if your debts are below £32000, you should expect to pay a minimum of £300 per month. Where your debts are higher than £32000, you would need to contribute more. An exception to this rule is when you have an available lump sum that can be contributed towards your IVA, perhaps by releasing equity from a property – in such a case, your monthly payment may be reduced. It is important to remember that from the creditor's point of view, you are agreeing to offer them as much as you can afford – not simply paying the minimum and keeping any extra money to yourself! Therefore, a Debt Advisor would sit down with you and work out exactly how much money you could realistically spare each month – no more and no less – and that would be the amount you would offer towards your IVA. Your case would be subject to annual review, and if your circumstances change for better or worse over the period of your IVA, you are obliged to contact your Insolvency Practitioner as soon as possible. Your case would be reassessed, and your payment plan may be adjusted accordingly. This is called 'variation'.

It is important to note that your Debt Advisor will view your monthly spending realistically when working out how much your

IVA payments will be. They will be careful to leave you enough to live on, without cutting any corners. The reason for this is that if you make dramatic cutbacks in your spending, it is unlikely that you will be able to maintain such a frugal lifestyle for the period of the IVA. If an emergency happens and you are left with an unforeseen expense, you may start to miss payments and your IVA may be at risk of failing, which could then lead to you being declared bankrupt. Remember – even if you feel sure that you can maintain a frugal lifestyle, your creditors may not agree. Therefore it is important to be honest and realistic when assessing your finances in the initial stages. If you would like to carry out this assessment yourself before speaking with a Debt Advisor, you can use the budget-sheet that is included in the Appendix at the back of this book.

Q I have my own company – do I qualify for an IVA?

A Absolutely. If you are the Director of a Limited Company, you are unable to declare bankruptcy and retain your position; therefore the IVA is specifically designed for your situation. If you are a sole trader, you may either go bankrupt or do an IVA without changing your occupation. If you decide to propose an IVA, you will need to present your business accounts, tax and VAT returns and trading projections to your Insolvency Practitioner. It is important that you are up-to-date with your tax calculations because the Inland Revenue will take a close look at your affairs if you propose an IVA. If you owe the Inland Revenue money, you must include them on the list of creditors on your IVA proposal.

Q Can I do an IVA together with my partner?

A If both you and your partner have unmanageable debts, it is possible for you both to propose an IVA simultaneously. Both of your cases will be read together, and a decision will be made on them both together. Thus you are not making a joint proposal, but two separate proposals that are linked and considered side-by-side.

Q I am on Income Support – do I qualify for an IVA?

A Legally, there is no reason why people on Income Support and other benefits cannot propose IVAs. In practice, however, if benefits are your sole income, the creditors are prone to reject such proposals because they do not have confidence in your ability to meet the repayments over the entire IVA period. Additionally, many creditors feel that it is morally wrong to accept an IVA from someone whose income is derived from benefits alone. The only exception to this is if you own a property that has equity in it. In such a case an IVA may have be possible because of the need to protect your house, which may otherwise be lost through bankruptcy.

Q How will an IVA affect my credit rating?

A There's no two ways about it: your credit rating will suffer if you undertake an IVA. The record of the IVA will remain on your credit file for 6 years, meaning that during this time you will be unable to take significant unsecured credit. Also, if you want to take a mortgage you will be subject to higher interest rates, and you may need to find a larger deposit than usual. If you are a first-time buyer and considering getting a mortgage, I would strongly advise you to wait until your IVA has come to an end. The reason for this is that in a worst case scenario, if your IVA fails and you are made bankrupt, you haven't so much to lose if you are not a homeowner. However, if you have just put your name on a mortgage, that property itself will then be seized as part of the bankruptcy proceedings. Thus buying a new house when in an IVA means that you are suddenly at risk of losing your house if for any reason something goes wrong.

Q   What will happen if I already own a house?

A   In the case of bankruptcy, the title to your house will always be taken from you by the court (if there is no equity in the property, you may be able to buy back the deeds – see Chapter Two for more details). In contrast to this, an IVA will allow you to keep control of your home. However, you will need to demonstrate commitment to repaying your creditors by agreeing to release as much equity as you can and contributing this towards your debt. From your point of view this is advantageous as well, because it may make your payment plan shorter.

The equity from your property will be released either at the beginning or at the end of your IVA period; however, it is usually released at the end. When the time comes, a specialist mortgage advisor will help you release equity to offer to your creditors, and this will usually mark the end of your IVA. Typically, the release of equity will happen in the 4th or 5th year of the agreement.

Where there is a large amount of equity involved, the length of the IVA can sometimes be reduced even further. In exceptional circumstances a full and final settlement can be negotiated on equity release alone; but this obviously demands a large amount of equity, and only applies to people who are unable to contribute to a monthly payment plan.

An IVA equity release should never leave you in financial difficulties – this would be clearly absurd! You will be left with larger mortgage repayments, but these will always be affordable. The agreed figure of your IVA payment will act as the bench-mark for future mortgage repayments. This means that if you are paying £300 towards your IVA, then when equity is released and your IVA is finished, you will be left with new mortgage payments of not more than £300 – an amount you can definitely afford. In most cases, after equity has been released the mortgage payments will increase by less than the monthly IVA payments you were making.

It is worth bearing in mind that if you do not want to release the equity in your property, there is an alternative: if you can persuade a friend or family member to put forward the value of the equity, the creditors will accept this instead. The important thing from their point of view is that you offer them the lump-sum value of the equity in your property, but this money does not necessarily have to come from the property itself.

Q   What will happen to my car in an IVA?

A   Exceptionally valuable assets must be assessed on a case-by-case basis. Usually it is possible to keep possession of a car worth a reasonable amount, especially if it is required for work or family reasons. If your car is financed on a Hire Purchase, the outstanding balance cannot be included in the IVA because it is a secured debt and the finance company will simply repossess the car. More often than not, you can continue to make your HP payments once your IVA has been put in place. However, once the HP is completed, the extra money would usually then be added towards your existing IVA payments. In some cases it may be best to 'cut your losses' and return the car to the finance company straight away. If this leaves you with a debt to them, this can be included within the IVA.

Q   What will happen to my saving policies in an IVA?

A   If you have an endowment policy or a savings account, the savings will have to be released and offered to the creditors as part of the IVA agreement. The creditors will not accept an IVA proposal if you have a nest-egg that you are not willing to release! Pension funds will not be released. However, you may have to suspend your pension contributions for the period of the IVA in order to pay more money back to your creditors on a monthly basis. For further details, contact a professional Debt Advisor.

Q   Is an IVA better than bankruptcy?

A   The answer to this question depends on your circumstances. For homeowners, an IVA is usually the better option because it enables you to keep control of the property (so long as the equity is released). Also, those who work in the Armed Forces, Police Force, Company Directorships and various legal and financial positions, have no alternative; they absolutely must do an IVA because if they went bankrupt their jobs may be at risk.

If you are not a homeowner and your job is not at risk, the decision is a more subjective one. From a purely financial point of view, in these circumstances the reality is that you are better off going bankrupt. Bankruptcy involves a 3-year payment plan, whereas an IVA lasts for 5 years (when there is no property involved). So by going bankrupt, you are asked to pay back less. However, for many people there is more at stake than finances. Bankruptcy would involve your name being published in both the local paper and the London Gazette. Many people find this hugely unappealing and opt for the IVA, which is entirely private and discreet. Furthermore, an IVA enables you to clear your debts without 'running away' from them, and some people believe that it is wrong to declare yourself bankrupt when there is another option open to you. Other people, however, feel no moral obligation to their creditors at all and are simply looking to get rid of their debts as soon as they can.

In summary, I have found that if somebody has no property and their job is not put at risk through bankruptcy, whether they decide to do an IVA or go bankrupt usually depends on their gut feeling. An IVA means that your privacy is maintained and you have made every effort to pay your debts back, and that can give peace of mind – but bankruptcy will mean that you pay back less and will be free from monthly payments sooner rather than later.

Q How can I make sure my IVA proposal will be successful?

A Generally speaking, for an IVA to be accepted it must clearly be more beneficial to the creditors than bankruptcy. If this is the case, then even though an IVA may require the creditors to write off a lot of money, they usually feel that half a loaf of bread is better than no bread at all.

Whether your particular IVA is accepted, however, is a different question. Many people are surprised by the fact that the amount of IVA proposals that are rejected each year in the UK currently stands at 20–40%! However, different IVA companies have different success rates. My own company, Thomas Charles & Co Ltd, has a success rate of more than 99%. We have managed to achieve this record through a combination of a client-centred approach and professional excellence.

The success of your IVA is partially dependent on the quality of the company that represents you. When choosing an IVA company, one thing to look out for is how much contact you have with professionals. Some companies keep you at arm's length – they send you the IVA forms by post and get you to complete them on your own, and you may have no option but to deal with the Insolvency Practitioner by post as well. Some people find this 'distance IVA' attractive because it does provide a degree of anonymity. However, in my experience I have found that when clients are left to complete their own paperwork by themselves, they tend to make errors on what can be a rather complicated set of forms. Obviously, an IVA proposal with errors in it is not a good idea! I believe that this methodology is detrimental to the client. For this reason, at Thomas Charles & Co Ltd you will be assigned a personal Debt Advisor who is will fill in all the paperwork for you. They will be contactable 24 hours a day, and will always be there to answer any questions you might have. In addition to this, your Debt Advisor will be aware that it may be beneficial for you to have a face-to-face meeting with your

Insolvency Practitioner, so that you can make absolutely sure that the proposal is watertight before you proceed. We work with a network of Insolvency Practitioners across the UK, and they each have their own area of specialisation and expertise ranging from military cases and family law to Company Directorships and property legislation. This means that we will link you with the best IP for your particular case, who can offer exactly the right expert advice and support. This helps to ensure that any issues that may endanger your IVA proposal are fixed straight away – before your proposal is put forward to the creditors. This high level of professionalism gives your IVA the best possible chance of success, and is one of the key factors in maintaining our market-leading 99% IVA success rate.

It is worth bearing in mind that if your IVA is rejected, you will have to resort to an alternative solution such as a Debt Management Plan or Bankruptcy. Technically speaking, it is possible to propose an IVA a second time, but in order to do this there will have to be a substantial, material change to your proposal. Thus a second proposal invariably involves more stress, uncertainty and hassle from creditors than the first one. For these reasons, it is of critical importance that you give your IVA the highest possible chance of success by using the very best representation on the market. So when deciding on which company you will choose to represent you, my advice is to ask these questions:

1 Will I have a personal Debt Advisor who I can contact at any time?

2 Will my Debt Advisor help me to complete the paperwork?

3 Will there be an option of a face-to-face meeting with an experienced Insolvency Practitioner?

4 Will I be linked with an IP who is an expert in cases such as mine?

5 Will there be a 'plan B' if my IVA proposal is questioned by the creditors or rejected?

Q   What is an IVA going to cost?

A   IVA companies may charge for their services, but the way in which they structure their fees varies from company to company. Many people find that it is worthwhile to pay for a professional IVA company to handle their case, because this usually ensures a more solid IVA proposal and thus a better chance of success. However, as mentioned earlier, it is worth shopping around and comparing services and prices before you choose which company you employ to represent you.

The Insolvency Practitioner is paid for the work that they do – but this money comes from the creditors, not from you. The creditors set aside a portion of the money that you contribute, and pay it as fees to the Insolvency Practitioner. The Insolvency Practitioner charges two fees to the creditors – a 'Nominee Fee' and a 'Supervisor Fee'. The Nominee Fee is usually fixed at £1000–£3000, and is a fee due to Licensed Insolvency Practitioners for carrying out negotiations with the creditors. The Supervisor Fee funds the Insolvency Practitioner to manage your IVA each year. This amount is usually in the region of £500–£1200 per annum.

Again it is important to stress that you yourself do not directly make a payment to the Insolvency Practitioner; the creditors are responsible for meeting this fee, but they do so out of the money that you offer to them.

Q   Can I include debts to my family and friends on my IVA proposal?

A   If you owe money to your family and friends, under normal circumstances you must include them on your IVA proposal by law. This is because if you continue to pay them while in an IVA, this could be seen as a preferential payment to one creditor over the others. Furthermore, it is usually in your interests to include family or friends on the list of creditors, because as official creditors they will be given the option to vote as to whether your IVA is accepted or not (and one would expect them to vote to accept the proposal!). However, even though they are allowed to vote like the other creditors, your friends and family are not normally allowed to receive a share of the IVA revenue.

Q How do I propose an IVA?

A As explained above, if you are considering proposing an IVA, first it is a good idea to do some research and find an IVA company that you have confidence in. Once you have done this, the Debt Advisor you have decided to work with will lead you through the different stages of the IVA process. Different companies follow slightly different procedures when it comes to preparing an IVA proposal; below is a list of steps that we follow at Thomas Charles & Co Ltd.

1 Over the telephone, you and your Debt Advisor will go through a document called a 'Statement Of Affairs' (SOA). This is a detailed appraisal of your financial circumstances, and it may take about an hour to complete. Many other companies send you the document and ask you to complete it on your own. However, at Thomas Charles & Co Ltd we like to complete the paperwork together with you to ensure that it is filled in correctly and so that we can answer any queries that you have as we go along.

2 After the meeting, your Debt Advisor would help you to decide whether or not the IVA is right for you. If you decide to commit to the IVA, you may need to stop paying your creditors. There are two main reasons for this. Firstly, people who are considering proposing an IVA are usually in a position where the only way to pay some creditors is to borrow from others. This could be viewed as fraudulent. After all, if you are considering an IVA, clearly you are unable to pay the money back! Secondly, it is advisable not to be seen to be making preferential payments to certain creditors, for this may hamper the smooth progress of your IVA. It is usually

wiser to make no payments to anybody rather than to unfairly make payments to some creditors but not others. In some cases, however, you will be advised to continue making minimum token payments to your creditors until your IVA is in place. Your Debt Advisor will be able to suggest what course of action you should take.

3 If you are banking with one of your creditors, you may need to open a fresh account with a bank that is not one of your creditors. The reason for this is that once your bank receives the IVA proposal they may take steps to close your account or reduce the facilities that they offer you. They also have a 'right of offset', which means that they can dip into your account and claim money without your consent to offset the debts you owe them. Thus you should open a new current account with an alternative bank, and if this is not possible you should open a basic account. More information on this is explained later in this chapter, and also in Chapter 2.

4 A hard copy of your SOA will be posted out for you to sign off and return. You will also need to send us financial documentation as evidence of the information on your draft IVA proposal.

5 Once the Thomas Charles & Co Ltd office has verified your SOA against your documentation, an Insolvency Practitioner will get involved. The IP may then arrange a face-to-face meeting with you in order to finalise your IVA proposal and make sure you are both clear about the terms and absolutely happy to proceed. You will then sign the proposal document.

6 The IP will then put your proposal forward to your creditors, who will be given 2 weeks to respond. After this time, there will be a creditor's meeting, giving the creditors the opportunity to discuss your proposal (these days, however, it is rare for an actual creditors' meeting to take place; creditors usually prefer to vote by proxy through the post). At this time, your creditors may decide to accept, accept with modifications, or reject your IVA. If you have

proposed your IVA through a reputable IVA company and an experienced IP, there is every chance that your IVA will be accepted. Indeed, a good IP will not go to the lengths of proposing an IVA unless they are 99% confident that it will succeed. If the creditors demand modifications to your proposal, your IP will work with you to negotiate a win-win settlement. However, at this point it must be noted that if your IVA is rejected, you are back to square one (you will not be automatically forced into bankruptcy).

7 Once your IVA is agreed, you must then carry out your side of the bargain and maintain your agreed payments. You must keep the IP informed if any of your circumstances change; if those changes are substantial, a variation proposal may need to be drafted and proposed once again to the creditors. During the period of your IVA you will certainly be subject to a level of financial restriction. However, when the IVA is over you will have no debt, no angry creditors and no financial restrictions whatsoever; after a year or two even your credit rating will be fully repaired. Thus, an IVA allows you to turn over a new leaf with your debts safely behind you. For many people, an IVA is a real life changing experience – without it, their situation would have been very difficult indeed.

Q   How do the creditors make their decision?

A   For an IVA to be successful, a majority of the creditors who decide to vote at the creditor's meeting need to accept the proposal. It will then be legally binding on the others, even if they refuse. To be more precise: an IVA proposal will be put in place if 75% of the value of the creditors who respond accept it. This means that if the major creditors do not bother to respond and only a handful of minor creditors vote at the Creditors' Meeting, their decision will be final and the larger creditors will be legally obliged to accept the IVA as well. For this reason, if you have a greater number of creditors, or friends and family creditors who are likely to vote within the given timescales, your IVA proposal will have a better chance of success (although in reality there is no reason why you shouldn't propose an IVA even if you only have a single creditor).

Q After my IVA has been agreed, can my creditors change their minds?

A Once the creditors have accepted the proposal at the Creditors' Meeting, they cannot pull out or renegotiate the terms because the IVA is a formal, legally-binding arrangement. This is one major benefit of an IVA compared to Debt Management Plans, where the creditors can alter their position whenever they feel like it (see Chapter 3).

Q What will happen if my IVA is accepted, but I have forgotten to include a creditor?

A If you fail to include a particular creditor in your and plan to continue to pay them separately without declaring it, this is in fact against the law as you are seen to be giving preferential treatment to a creditor. The IVA paperwork specifically requires you to sign a statement that declares that you have no other creditors, so if this is not the case, it may cause a significant problem. However, this does not mean that the IVA will automatically fail; if you have made a genuine mistake, there are ways of pulling it back from the brink. Essentially, the best route forward would have to be decided between you and your Insolvency Practitioner. You would need to approach your IP and explain what has happened, and he or she will then decide what to do. If the extra creditor is not major, an addition may be made to the IVA list and things will proceed as before. However, if the new debt reduces the overall creditor dividend by 10% or more, the case will have to be reopened, the Creditors' Meeting reconvened, and the creditors will be called upon to vote again. In a worst case scenario, the IVA may fail and you would be put at risk of being made bankrupt.

Q   When will my creditors stop hassling me?

A   Once the IVA is in place, the creditors can no longer contact you by law, and you will be left to live a quiet life. However, in order to proceed with an IVA, most people need to stop paying their creditors first. There are two reasons for this. Firstly, as mentioned above, to borrow more money when you intend to do an IVA could be regarded as fraudulent, so if paying creditors means borrowing more money, the best thing to do is stop making payments. Secondly, it is generally unwise to be seen to be making preferential, unfair payments to certain creditors and not others. For this reason, it is better to stop your payments altogether than pay some creditors and not others.

Once you have stopped paying the creditors, they will begin the usual debt collection procedure – 'snotty letters' will arrive, and possibly phone calls as well. Unfortunately there is not much that can be done about this. However, there is light at the end of the tunnel; once your IVA is in place, creditor action must stop and your creditors will be legally prevented from contacting you. For this reason, you should help the IP to move as quickly as possible by doing all you can to collect the required paperwork together as soon as you can.

Q   What will happen if my financial position changes over the IVA period?

A   Realistically speaking, financial circumstances may vary over the IVA period, and allowances can be made for unexpected events. For example, if you are suddenly made redundant, the first thing you would do would be to notify your Insolvency Practitioner. Your Insolvency Practitioner would then arrange a 'payment holiday' for you, allowing you to get yourself back on your feet before resuming your IVA payments (missed payments will be added to the end of the agreement). If a more serious emergency arises, for example a period of prolonged unemployment, it may be possible to propose a variation of your IVA to your creditors which they will be asked to accept. If this variation is reasonable, there is no reason why the creditors should not comply. It is important to bear in mind that you are agreeing to pay whatever you can comfortably afford to your creditors, so if this amount changes drastically, your IVA will certainly be affected. During your IVA period you should be left with a reasonable amount of money to live on, but you will not be living in the lap of luxury. If your IVA is professionally handled and your personal records are in an organised state, there's no reason why it should not go smoothly.

Q What if I receive a sudden windfall, such as an inheritance, while in an IVA?

A If you receive a large lump sum or inheritance while you are in an IVA, you will need to contribute it towards your debts. If it adds up to more than your total IVA contribution, you will pay back more to your creditors than first agreed; ultimately, you will be required to pay off all your original debt if you can afford to do so.

Q Can I have a bank account when I am in an IVA?

A In an IVA, you can hold either a basic account or a current account. If your present bank is one of your major creditors, you would be wise to open up a new account with another bank before your IVA is proposed. This is because if you owe money to your bank which is at risk of not being repaid, the banks may use their 'right of offset' to take money from your account without your consent to help repay your outstanding debt. Furthermore, once your bank receives your IVA proposal, they may reduce your current account to a basic account, or even close the account altogether. It is therefore best to pre-empt the situation and open a new account with an alternative bank. Since your IVA is a private and confidential arrangement, there is no way that your new bank would ever know that you are in an IVA unless you tell them. This means that your new account will not be at risk as a result of your IVA.

When faced with the option of having either a basic account or a current account, it is far more advantageous to have a current account, as with this account you will normally be issued with a debit card and cheque book. However, if your credit rating precludes the possibility of opening a full current account, you will normally still be able to open a basic cash card account. This is a simple account with no lending facilities. It is less convenient than a current account as you do not usually get a debit card. However, it is clearly better than no account at all!

When you are looking for a new bank or building society, you should make sure that it is not linked to any bank you owe money to, like Halifax and the Bank of Scotland, for example, who are part of the same organisation. More information about managing basic accounts can be found in Chapter Two.

Finally, it is worth mentioning that if you are a self-employed sole trader and have a business account with a creditor, the best advice would be to open up a new business account with somebody else. This is because all the dangers mentioned above apply equally to your business account when you propose an IVA. If you find it impossible to open a new business account because of your bad credit rating, there may be an option to leave your bank debt out of the IVA so that you can continue to run your business. However, this can only work if they are not a primary creditor. If your credit rating is bad and your bank is a primary creditor, it may be difficult to propose an IVA whilst maintaining your business activities.

Q   What to do next?

A   If you think that an IVA may be right for you, the first thing to do would be to seek professional advice from a reputable IVA company such as Thomas Charles & Co Ltd. You can contact Thomas Charles & Co Ltd on 0870 141 72 71 or at www.thomascharles.com. Once you have found a company that you feel comfortable with, they will lead you through the necessary steps detailed above until your

IVA is in place. The main thing is to make absolutely sure that the people dealing with your IVA are professional and have a good track record. I have already explained the kind of questions you need to ask them to ascertain whether or not your IVA is in the best possible hands. If you choose a good company and they handle your IVA well, you should be well on the way to becoming debt-free – there will finally be light at the end of the tunnel.

Case Study

Marion and David were both working in full time jobs. Marion was a Travel Agent, and David worked as a Recruitment Consultant. Together, they brought back around £3700 per month. They saw credit facilities as useful ways of getting goods up front, and they never had any problems managing repayments. They had a store card, two credit cards and a personal loan, which had been used to buy a car. In addition, they were making mortgage payments. But they never ran into any difficulties meeting these. They enjoyed a reasonable lifestyle – going out with friends, eating in restaurants, and at least two holidays a year.

Their financial difficulties began when they had their first child. Marion minimised her income gap by working until the last minute – she began her maternity leave only 2 weeks before her child was born. However, it was a complicated birth and Marion ended up spending several weeks recovering in hospital. Her income fell to statutory maternity pay. This meant that the monthly household income was reduced by £600. In addition, David had to take time off work to look after her and the baby in hospital. To make matters worse, the day-to-day costs of petrol and parking in the hospital car-park put them under extra financial strain. David decided to supplement their income by using credit cards. He did not feel that there would be an issue with repayment as he believed that Marion would return to her full time job. The credit cards were merely a convenient way to see them through – a stop-gap measure. However, due to complications with her health, Marion was only able to go back to work part-time. This meant that money was extremely tight, especially now that there were additional child minding costs and an extra mouth to feed. Things started to spiral out of control.

For the next 18 months, Marion and David tried to juggle their debts by taking consolidation loans. However, every month they were forced to rob Peter to pay Paul and soon their monthly repayments increased to more than £900 – way more than they could ever possibly afford. Something had to be done to stop the situation from getting any worse. They began to fear that they were heading for bankruptcy – and Marion in particular felt that she couldn't cope with losing the house.

With specialist advice from Thomas Charles & Co Ltd, Marion and David decided to undertake an IVA. Through this arrangement, they have agreed an affordable payment plan with their creditors. Their debts will be cleared in a few years, and they are able to keep their house. The constant telephone calls and payment demand letters have stopped. Finally, they have been able to get their lives back on track. They were so pleased that they have since referred no less than four friends to Thomas Charles & Co Ltd to benefit from IVAs! As Marion put it, 'once the IVA is complete we are going to save up and take a nice, long holiday – on our own money.'

Chapter Two

Bankruptcy

The Bankruptcy Act was first instituted in 1571. Originally, only traders and craftsmen could be declared bankrupt; everyone else would be imprisoned if they didn't pay their debts. As you would imagine, this meant that everyone in financial difficulties tried to qualify as traders in order to avoid the debtors' prison! This situation was revised in 1861, when all insolvent debtors were allowed to petition for bankruptcy. This arrangement has been standing ever since, meaning that today anyone in a position of insolvency can declare themselves bankrupt. Furthermore, in 2004 a number of changes were made to bankruptcy law in the much-publicised 'Enterprise Act'. One effect of this was that the duration of bankruptcy has been reduced. Prior to the amendments, bankrupts would be discharged after two or three years; now they are discharged after only twelve months.

Bankruptcy can be forced upon you by creditors who are owed a minimum of £750, if you have repeatedly defaulted on your payments to them. It can also be forced upon you if you undertake an IVA and then fail to make the monthly payments. However, you can also choose to declare yourself bankrupt voluntarily, which many people feel allows them a certain degree of dignity.

What is Bankruptcy?

Bankruptcy is a method of dealing with debts which you can not possibly repay. It is normally seen as a last resort, after all other options for dealing with debt have been exhausted. If you declare yourself bankrupt, the responsibility for repaying your debts is removed and the court will prevent any further creditor actions against you. You are usually bankrupt for only twelve months, during which time you are subject to various restrictions: you cannot take out a mortgage, be a company director, take a position in the police force or military, or be employed in various professional positions. Your 'Bankruptcy Order' will usually be accompanied by an 'Income Payment Order', meaning that you will have to make payments to the court over a period of 3 years if you can afford to do so. During that time, you will be unable to save money or enjoy an expensive lifestyle. Most importantly, if you go bankrupt you will lose control of your assets – your house may be at risk if there is equity in it (although it may not be physically repossessed for 12 months), and so will your car if it is worth more than £1500. These assets will be seized by the court and shared between your creditors.

Generally, it is wise to consider every avenue before opting for bankruptcy. Bankruptcy is a serious matter, so you should thoroughly research IVAs, Informal Repayment Plans and Loan Consolidations to make sure that you are making an informed decision. Having said that, for some people bankruptcy is the answer – it can provide an effective solution to overwhelming debt problems.

Bankruptcy: the advantages

- All of your debts will be taken away from you and you will no longer be responsible for repaying them.

- After twelve months you will be 'discharged' from bankruptcy, and the bankruptcy restrictions will be lifted. Any money outstanding will be written off, except for Student Loan Company debts and non-dischargeable debts.

- Even though your house and car may be at risk, your reasonable household goods are safe – nobody will be knocking on your door to seize your DVD player, sofa, fridge or washing machine (unless they are exceptionally valuable).

- Your payment plan to the court usually lasts for a maximum of three years – that's two years less than an IVA.

Bankruptcy: the disadvantages

- You will usually lose control of your house.

- Although you will be able to keep reasonable household items and cars worth less than £1500, any asset above this may be lost (unless it is reasonably required in the course of your business).

- Bankruptcy is a public affair; your name will be published both in your local newspaper and the London Gazette.

- You will be required to pay any extra money that you have to the court, usually for three years.

- Your credit rating is significantly damaged; the record of your bankruptcy will remain on your credit file for six years.

- Debts to the Student Loans Company cannot be included, and will remain after you have been discharged.

Moreover, whilst bankrupt you cannot:

- Obtain credit for over £250 without informing the lender you are bankrupt.

- Be a Company Director, or be involved in the promotion, formation or management of a limited company without permission from the court.

- Trade in any business under a different name unless all persons involved are informed of your bankruptcy.

- Practice as a Lawyer, Chartered Accountant, or work within financial services or jobs involving substantial responsibility.

- Become a Member of Parliament, Justice Of The Peace or Local Authority member.

- Join the Police Force or military.

Clearly, then, the decision to declare yourself bankrupt can involve substantial consequences. However, if you find that these consequences do not greatly affect you – or if you are unable to deal with your debts in any other way – bankruptcy may be the right choice.

Questions and Answers

Q Who should go bankrupt?

A By and large, most homeowners who declare bankruptcy have no alternative. They would usually have tried informal solutions such as Informal Repayments and Debt Consolidation, and found that their problems remain unsolved. They might also have considered the possibility of an IVA, and found that they could not afford the repayments that it requires. Once all these options are exhausted, the only thing left to do is go bankrupt, and resign themselves to the probability of losing their house.

Non-homeowners, however, are normally not affected as drastically by bankruptcy. They may even opt for bankruptcy over an IVA (which would ultimately be more expensive). This is particularly the case if their job would not be at risk, and they are not worried about having a devastated credit rating or having their name in the papers. Non-homeowners living on State Benefits or a pension would probably be discharged from bankruptcy in less than one year, and would probably not be subject to an Income Payment Order. For these people, then, bankruptcy is especially attractive.

You might feel uncomfortable about the idea of going bankrupt when there are other options available. However, the reality is that for non-homeowners bankruptcy is often the financially preferable alternative; you will usually be required to make payments for only three years, rather than the 60 payments that an IVA would usually require.

Q   Are there any debts that bankruptcy does not cover?

A   Debts are divided into 'dischargeable debts', which are covered by bankruptcy, and 'non-dischargeable debts', which are not. General guidelines are listed below.

Dischargeable debts include:

- Inland Revenue and VAT bills

- Unsecured loans

- Credit card debts

- Legal, Medical and Accounting bills

- Unpaid bills, including catalogue accounts and store cards

- County Court Judgements (CCJ's)

Non-dischargeable debts include:

- Debts to the Student Loans Company

- Fines and penalties

- Secured debts and loans with collateral

- CSA claims for child support and other family/domestic legal liabilities

- Most educational loans which fall outside of the Insolvency Act 1986

Q   How long will bankruptcy last?

A   Although bankruptcy usually lasts for just one year, the length of your bankruptcy ultimately lies at the discretion of the Official Receiver. The Official Receiver may conclude the case early if your main income is State Benefit or a Pension, if your debts and expenses have been fully paid, or if the order shouldn't have been made in the first place. On the other hand, if you fail to meet the bankruptcy terms, if you have been bankrupt previously, or if you have engaged in fraud, gambling or other related activities, the Official Receiver may increase the duration of your Bankruptcy Order for up to ten years.

Q   Can I go bankrupt more than once?

A   Yes. However, if you declare bankruptcy a second time, the period of your Bankruptcy Order is likely to be extended and your Income Payment Order may be extended too.

Q   Can I have a bank account if I go bankrupt?

A   If you go bankrupt, you can still hold a bank account – but not a regular Current Account. Instead you would have a basic account, which usually means no lending facilities, cheque book or debit card. Unfortunately, not all banks and building societies will offer this account to people who are bankrupt. The best advice would be to contact the Financial Services Authority, who should be able to assist you with detailed information about basic accounts. With enough research you should be able to find a bank who will offer you a basic account, and you may even be able to open a basic account with a Solo or Electron Debit Card facility.

Generally speaking, however, a basic account means that you would have no significant overdraft or lending facilities, no cheque book and no debit card. Clearly this is a hassle, as it means that you have to pay for all your transactions with cash. One helpful hint might be to consider using a new type of Debit Card called a 'Pre-payment Debit Card', which has been recently introduced in the UK. This is based on the concept of 'charging up' a Debit Card with money, and then using the money on that card for transactions and purchases. There are currently a handful of companies who supply these cards in the UK, but this is likely to increase. There is normally a monthly charge for using such a card, which would typically be around £5 per month.

Q   What costs are involved in going bankrupt?

A   To go bankrupt voluntarily, there is a one-off charge of £460 - £500 in court fees. In addition to this, the Official Receiver will assess your financial position, and you may be required to contribute monthly payments to the court in the form of an Income Payment Order. The amount you pay each month will be linked to the amount you can afford, so you will definitely still have enough to live on. Your Income Payment Order will normally last for 3 years; it is unlikely to run for longer unless the Official Receiver feels there is a substantial reason to prolong it such as evidence of fraud or a previous bankruptcy.

Q   How does bankruptcy affect my credit rating?

A   During the bankruptcy period itself (normally 12 months), you will find it extremely difficult to get a mortgage or any form of unsecured credit. After you are discharged it will become increasingly possible to borrow again. However, as mentioned above, there can be nothing more damaging for your credit rating than bankruptcy. It remains on your credit file for six years, meaning that for this period it is very difficult for you to obtain further unsecured credit without being subject to significantly increased interest. Although there are an ever increasing number of adverse mortgage brokers who work with individuals who have been discharged from bankruptcy, you will be unable to take secured credit at normal rates. On the other hand, some people may feel that an incentive not to borrow money would be a blessing in disguise!

Q   What happens if I come into some money?

A   If you happen to receive a lump sum during the 12 months of your bankruptcy, this money must be declared to the court and may be seized for the purposes of paying your creditors. However, once you have been discharged you are allowed to keep any lump sums you receive, even though your Income Payment Order may still run for a further two years.

Q   What will happen to my pension fund?

A   In most cases, your pension fund would remain untouched by the court. However, you may be required to suspend payments into the fund for the duration of your bankruptcy.

Q   Will somebody knock on my door and take away everything I own?

A   The short answer is no. Don't worry about men arriving outside your house with a white van and taking all of your worldly goods, leaving you sitting on an orange-box. The only assets that may be seized are houses, cars worth more than £1500, and household items that are not seen to be reasonable. As a rule of thumb, the law states that if you sell an expensive item and receive enough money to buy a cheaper replacement with a substantial amount left over, that item would be classed as 'unreasonable' and it would have to be disposed of and the proceeds contributed towards your bankruptcy. Such items might include a plasma television or a state-of-the-art sound system. If you don't possess any such luxurious items, you will be safe from the bailiffs.

Q   What happens if my property is in joint name?

A   If you have a joint mortgage, the title would be seized regardless of your partner's financial situation. Unfortunately, there is no way to avoid this forced sale. However, the court will only be able to claim your share of the equity; the rest of the equity will be returned to its rightful owner. Your partner would, however, be able to make an offer to buy your share of the equity and this money would be offered to the Official Receiver instead.

Q What will happen if I have no equity in my property?

A The creditors are not interested in the physical bricks and mortar of your house – what they want is the equity that is tied up in it. If your house contains no equity at all, the Official Receiver will still take possession of the house. However, once this has happened, I would strongly advise you to approach the Official Receiver and offer to buy back the title to the property for a nominal sum of £1 (plus the cost of solicitor's fees). If you fail to do this, the Official Receiver will remain in control of the property for 3 years. If the property has acquired more value during that time, you would stand to lose that money. However, if the Official Receiver does not sell the property within 3 years, the Enterprise Act states that the property would be returned to you.

Q Can I save my assets by signing them over into somebody else's name?

A Absolutely not. The court will check as to whether you have given away any major assets – or sold them for less than their true value – over the last five years. If you have done so, the asset may be seized by the court regardless of who is in control of it at that time.

Q Can I borrow extra money to clear someone else's debts and then go bankrupt myself?

A No. If you have done this, the court will view it as giving away assets (as above). The money will be sought out by the court and seized, and the person you helped will be back where they started.

Q Will my partner be affected by my bankruptcy?

A In terms of their job and other aspects of life, the answer is no; if your financial affairs are separate, your partner will not be affected by your bankruptcy in the least. However, in terms of your partner's credit rating, there can sometimes be consequences – but these can be avoided. It is common for information to creep from one person's credit file to another's, especially if you share the same address. In order to prevent this from happening, you can contact the UK credit file companies Experian and Equifax and ask them to 'create a disassociation'. This means that your information will be removed from their file, and their information removed from yours. To do this, you must give Experian or Equifax your full names and dates of birth, as well as details of your relationship and any shared addresses.

Q   What to do next?

A   If you think that bankruptcy is right for you, the first thing to do would be to seek professional advice from either the Citizens Advice Bureaux or a reputable Debt Consultancy service such as Thomas Charles & Co Ltd. Once you have decided that bankruptcy is the correct way forward and have understood all the associated issues, you should contact your local County Court (or the High Court if you live in London). You can find their details in the phone book. The court will provide you with a bankruptcy form, and all the further information you need. The form is complex and the court will not help you to complete it. There are various companies that can assist you in doing so, including Thomas Charles & Co Ltd. Once your form has been completed you must take it in person to the court, and the court fees will be payable at that time. You will be asked to meet with a District Judge, and if they believe you are insolvent and bankruptcy is the right option for you, a Bankruptcy Order can be issued on the same day. After this, you will meet with a member of the Official Receiver's office to discuss the terms and details of your Bankruptcy Order, including the length of the bankruptcy, the details of the Income Payment Order and the issues involved with asset liquidation.

Case Study

Mr Percival was born in South Africa, but immigrated to the UK when he married his wife, a British citizen. The move inevitably involved significant expenses. While he and his wife were getting themselves up and running, Mr Percival found himself turning to credit cards to pay his way. They rented a property in London, and both found jobs without difficulty – Mr Percival was working as a hotel manager, and Mrs Percival as a PA. Initially Mr Percival found his credit card repayments manageable, and this situation continued for a couple of years.

Unfortunately, in 2005 Mr Percival was made redundant. He was unemployed for several months, and during this time his credit card bills crept up and up. Eventually he found a new job in a catering company, but this involved taking a significant pay cut. Nevertheless, there was an option of overtime and weekend work, and Mr Percival found that he could just afford his credit card repayments through careful budgeting, hard work and a frugal lifestyle. Things were tough, but he struggled on. With time, however, credit card balances began to gradually rise again, and Mr Percival found himself working more and more overtime. In mid-2006, he took a consolidation loan, and hoped that this would solve the problem.

Not long afterwards, Mr Percival's overtime dried up without warning. He found it harder and harder to make ends meet, and began robbing Peter to pay Paul using new credit cards. Eventually he was forced to take a second job as a waiter in a local restaurant. However, by this time his debts had grown so large that the minimum repayments outweighed his income.

Something had to be done. First of all, Mr Percival considered enacting an IVA and contacted a professional debt Advisor at Thomas Charles & Co Ltd. However, the Debt Advisor was not confident that Mr Percival would be able to comfortably afford the IVA repayments. Since his debts were so high and his salary wasn't huge, the Debt

Advisor felt that an IVA would be impossible. An additional factor was the fact that the Mr Percival did not own a home, or own an expensive car. Furthermore, his new job would not be put at risk through bankruptcy, and even though his name would appear in the local newspaper, this was not really a concern for him living in London. The Debt Advisor suggested that Mr Percival would be better off going bankrupt.

Mr Percival felt uncomfortable about going bankrupt at first. However, his Debt Advisor emailed him some detailed information on bankruptcy, and when he looked at the facts on paper, he decided that it wasn't going to be so bad after all. He contacted the local court and was declared bankrupt shortly afterwards. All his debts were taken off his shoulders, and he felt confident to move on. He is now putting money aside each month so that in a few years' time he can retire in his native South Africa.

Chapter Three

Debt Management Plan

Debt Management Plans have existed for as long as people have been borrowing money. They basically mean that the debtor appeals to the creditor and requests that the minimum monthly payment is reduced. These arrangements are informal – they are made on the basis of a 'gentleman's agreement', and are not legally binding. This means that there are no solicitors or legal representatives involved. All you have to do is contact your creditors, explain your situation and request them to show mercy. There are a variety of commercial Debt Management companies on the market who will undertake these negotiations for you, in return for a sizeable commission. Alternatively, there are non-profit-making organisations such as the Citizens Advice Bureaux (CAB) and the Consumer Credit Counselling Service (CCCS) who will help you put a Debt Management Plan in place for free. Debt Management Plans are fairly common these days amongst people who are in serious debt. But can they really solve your debt problems?

What is a Debt Management Plan?

A Debt Management Plan is a way of getting your monthly payments – but not your total debt – reduced. This can sometimes be an effective solution. For many people, the main problem is that they cannot meet all their minimum payments each month. This means that they start 'robbing Peter to pay Paul' – borrowing money from one creditor in order to pay another. This situation should be avoided at all costs. It is a 'slippery slope' that only leads to more and more debt and eventually even to bankruptcy. Even though it might appear that you are keeping your head above water because you are not missing payments, in reality this is deceptive; clearly, making payments by borrowing money can only make matters worse in the long run. By contacting your creditors individually and explaining your difficulties, you may be able to persuade them to temporarily reduce your minimum payments. This can sometimes work very well, because reduced minimum payments can allow you to pay your creditors without having to resort to robbing Peter to pay Paul. In this way you can solve the most pressing problem – you can stop borrowing more money. But it is important to recognise that you may not have found an effective solution to your debts as a whole.

When agreeing to a Debt Management Plan, your creditors are reducing your minimum payments, NOT your total debt. In actual fact, such a plan may cause your total debt to increase – by reducing your payments it will take longer to clear your debts, which means you may end up paying much more interest. The creditors are under no legal obligation to freeze interest charges; so even though some creditors may agree to freeze interest for a while, this may not be for ever and may not make much difference in the long-term. In some cases it is possible for the interest to end up accumulating at a faster rate than you are paying it off! So you will often find that there is no end in sight as your debt may actually be growing rather than reducing. Moreover, since your agreement is not legally binding, the creditors are at liberty to review your case at any time and demand higher payments. This means that you will never know when the goal-posts will be moved, and you run the risk of your finances being destabilised at short notice. Your creditors may change their minds and start charging interest again, or they might suddenly demand the full amount to be paid a few months down the line. Additionally, even though your creditors agree a reduced monthly payment, you will still be penalised for not paying the full amount each month. This means that default notices may still be issued against you, and your credit rating will remain poor until the total debt is paid – which could take a very long time.

Debt Management Plan: the advantages

- Reducing your monthly payments may enable you to avoid robbing Peter to pay Paul and put a stop to your borrowing.

- Coming to a temporary arrangement with creditors is generally looked upon more favourably than missing payments to them. However, they may still continue to chase you for their money.

Debt Management Plan: the disadvantages

- Your credit rating will remain damaged until all your debts have been repaid; default notices may still be issued.

- Interest is unlikely to be frozen by all creditors, which means that you may end up paying back much more money over a far longer period.

- There is no end in sight. Even if interest is frozen on some debts, reduced monthly payments will always mean a greatly extended payback period so it will take you longer to get debt-free.

- There is no peace of mind. Any agreement you reach is not legally binding, so the creditors are at liberty to change their minds at any time, change their interest charges, or demand that you resume full payments to them.

Questions and Answers

Q   Who should use a Debt Management Plan?

A   This solution is more likely to suit people who owe less than £15000 because it is usually possible to repay such amounts in full in a reasonable period of time in a Debt Management Plan. If your debts are greater than that, however, you should seriously think about enacting either an IVA or bankruptcy. The main reason for this is that if you simply reduce the repayments on large debts, you may end up paying them off for the rest of your life! So you probably need a solution that will allow some of them to be written off. Whatever your level of debt, if your financial position is due to improve in the near future as a result of an income increase or a re-mortgage and you are looking for a way to tread water until then, the Debt Management Plan could be the best solution for you because it temporarily maintains the status quo (although your credit rating may be damaged in the process).

Debt Management Plans tend not to work for people with a large number of different creditors. This is because it is almost impossible to negotiate effectively with many different creditors at once – even if one creditor agrees, others may not. Once an agreement has been reached, the negotiations are not over – you may find yourself having to re-negotiate with the same creditor a few months down the line. As such, if you have a large number of different creditors, negotiating agreements with all of them can be a time-consuming nightmare! In my experience, I have found that many people tend to lose track of the different arrangements they have made. This leads them to miss payments simply because they find it difficult to manage a variety of small repayment agreements. Using a Debt Management company to carry out negotiations on your behalf can help to an extent, but there are significant disadvantages involved (Debt Management companies are discussed fully below). For these reasons I would usually recommend a self-managing Debt Management Plan to people who are extremely well-organised, or who have a total of 5 creditors or less.

By now it will be very apparent that in the vast majority of cases, Debt Management Plans are not long-term solutions. However, at the very least, they can allow some breathing space from your creditors while you concentrate on trying to increase your earnings. In other words, this solution usually works best as a stop-gap.

Q   How can I set up a Debt Management Plan?

A   The best way to put a Debt Management Plan in place is first of all to sit down and compile a list of exactly how much money you owe to each creditor, inclusive of interest and all charges. You can find out roughly how much is owed on your loans by multiplying your normal monthly payment by the amount of months that you have left to pay. Having done this, you should calculate what percentage of the total debt is owed to each individual creditor. Then, using the budget-sheet at the back of this book, you should draw up a budget sheet for your personal monthly income and expenses, and come up with a sum of money that you feel you could realistically offer to your creditors each month. This is called your 'disposable income'. You should divide your disposable income between the creditors on a pro rata basis, allocating each creditor a portion equivalent to their percentage of the total debt. For example, let's say you have a disposable income of £300, and your total debt is comprised of £3000 to Lloyds TSB, £3000 to HSBC, £1500 to Halifax and £1500 to Cahoot. This will mean that Lloyds TSB and HSBC can both be reasonably allocated 33.3% of your disposable income, and Halifax and Cahoot could be offered 16.6% each. Thus your £300 disposable income would be split up as follows: £100 to Lloyds TSB (33.3%), £100 to HSBC (33.3%), £50 to Halifax (16.6%) and £50 to Cahoot (16.6%). This calculation will form the basis of your negotiations, and you should make this clear in the letter that you write to the creditors and your further discussions with them.

As an additional rule of thumb, you should be looking to pay a minimum of at least 1% of your total debt to each creditor every month in order to stand any chance of getting a freeze put on interest. If this amount is unaffordable, you might need to consider one of the other options described in this book.

Q   Should I use a Debt Management company?

A   If you believe a Debt Management Plan is right for you, your best course of action would probably be to get professional support for free, through the Citizens Advice Bureaux (CAB) or Consumer Credit Counselling Service (CCCS). At the moment, there are many commercial Debt Management companies vying with one another to sign people up and deal with their finances on their behalf. On the whole, I would advise against using such companies. The reason for this is that Debt Management companies take a commission for doing a task that you could essentially do for free, either on your own or through the CCCS or CAB. These commissions are usually around 17.5% plus VAT, and in my view this money would be better spent on the debt itself rather than sinking it into the coffers of a Debt Management company. It is very tempting to hand over the controls of your financial affairs to somebody else and simply make a monthly payment to them which they share between your creditors on your behalf. This is especially true if your finances are in a shambles and you're not sure how much you owe and to whom. However, you carefully should weigh up the potential benefits against the additional costs. Otherwise you may be in danger of finding yourself several years down the line having paid a Debt Management company a lot of money but with nothing other than a larger debt to show for it. I have lost track of the number of clients I have helped to do an IVA or go bankrupt whose problems have been compounded through hastily signing up with a Debt Management company. Therefore, it is wise to be cautious when dealing with such organisations. Here is a list of important questions to ask them:

1 How long will it take me to get debt-free?

2 What exactly will I be paying in commission each month?

3 Is there any guarantee that my creditors will freeze interest and charges?

4 Will I receive monthly statements and full notification of how my affairs are being managed?

When asking these questions, make sure you get clear and accurate information. Bear in mind that the creditors are under no legal obligation to negotiate with Debt Management companies; indeed, often creditors resent such companies for taking a payment for themselves while advising people to reduce debt repayments! Essentially, there is not much these companies can do that you cannot do yourself with enough time and energy, and the creditors have no particular legal requirement or incentive to deal with a third party rather than you. Furthermore it is important to understand that creditors are under no legal obligation whatsoever to freeze interest and charges. Debt Management companies are often optimistic that they will be able to persuade creditors to do this, but the harsh reality is that it is by no means guaranteed. Some creditors might begrudgingly agree to freeze interest for a while, but there is no telling how long this will last.

In summary, then, I would advise you to only employ a Debt Management company when you are absolutely unable to deal with the situation yourself, or strongly do not want the hassle involved in doing so. Be prepared for a long-term repayment period that may not necessarily lead you to debt freedom. The most important question to ask them is the first on the list above: How long will it take me to get debt-free?

Q   What to do next?

A   If you are planning on putting a Debt Management Plan in place, the wisest course of action would be to take control of the situation and educate yourself in debt solutions so that you can make an informed decision yourself about what you want to do. If you would like a professional to represent you, you can contact the Citizens Advice Bureaux (CAB) or Consumer Credit Counselling Service (CCCS), who will give you as much help as you need for free. It is usually best to speak to them first, and then if you are still not satisfied, contact a commercial Debt Management Company. However, bear in mind that a commercial company may not be able to provide you with a better service, despite the charges they make.

If you choose to undertake the negotiations yourself, first you should complete the budget-sheet at the back of this book and arrive at a figure that represents your disposable income. Then work out how this would be shared fairly amongst your creditors on a pro-rata basis, as described above. Once you have drafted your proposal and worked out how much you are able to give to each creditor, you should contact them in writing, explaining your situation and putting forward your offer, including a request that they freeze all interest and charges. One useful tip is to cut up your credit card and slip it in with the letter; this will send the creditors the message that you definitely intend to stop running up debt. Your creditors will normally play hardball at first, and you may need to be persistent in negotiations before you are able to come to an agreement. Some creditors will simply refuse to negotiate, and others will be happy to compromise – but you will never know what the result will be until you give it a go.

Case Study

Hazel first began accumulating debt when she was working as a Receptionist in a Solicitor's firm in Southend-on-Sea. Initially, she was earning only £9000 per year. As a result of this low wage, she started relying on two credit cards to pay her way. This was soon followed by a bank loan and an overdraft. After a couple of years, her debts had mounted to £8000, and she was in a situation where every month she found herself robbing Peter to pay Paul.

Hazel decided to look for a new job as a PA, and found one fairy quickly, in London. Her salary was due to start at £12000, and rise to £15000 within six months. Within a year, her salary would increase to £20000. Even though this made her optimistic for the future, the future seemed a long way off. Hazel had to find a way to solve her problems now, as creditors were beginning to hassle her for money.

Initially, she couldn't see a way out of her predicament and thought the only solution for her was to go bankrupt. But then a friend told her about the possibility of doing an IVA, and she contacted a professional Debt Advisor at Thomas Charles & Co Ltd. The Debt Advisor analysed her situation, and informed her that because she only owed £8000, she did not qualify for an IVA. She was advised to consider a Debt Management Plan.

Hazel contacted her bank and her two credit card companies and managed to negotiate reduced monthly repayments based on an analysis of her monthly budget and a pro-rata assessment of her debts. As a result of this, she managed to avoid defaulting and robbing Peter to pay Paul. Six months later she got her pay-rise, and due to her increased income was able to once again increase the monthly payments to the original sum. She is now managing her finances very effectively, and is in a position to do so only thanks to her Debt Management Plan. The default notices issued during the time she spent in a Debt Management Plan mean that her credit rating is not as good as it used to be, but she has no intention of taking any more credit for a very long time anyway! Hazel is due to get married later in the year.

Chapter Four

Debt Consolidation

Debt consolidation has become increasingly popular in recent years. It is currently the biggest single reason why people take loans in the UK, and this does not look likely to change. Although debt can be consolidated through secured borrowing, many people choose to consolidate through unsecured credit, whether in the form of personal loans or credit card balance transfers. Debt consolidation can sometimes seem to be the perfect solution, but it can be an extremely risk business; if not done properly it can often land you in greater debt difficulties and make the problem worse.

What is Debt Consolidation?

Debt Consolidation means clearing your existing debts with a new single credit facility such as a personal loan. The principle behind debt consolidation is that the more individual debts you have, the more expensive it will be and the harder it will become to keep on top of your repayments. As such, if you consolidate your debts into a single place, this can lower interest and make it much easier to manage your repayments. Ideally, you should aim to be left with just one, single debt that you are confident you can afford to pay. The money you owe hasn't gone away – it is just in a different place, and this means that you don't have the stress and complications involved with maintaining multiple payments to a variety of creditors. It also means that your new, single repayment is likely to be lower than the amount you were paying out before in multiple payments.

If you are a homeowner, you may be able to release equity from your property in order to consolidate your debt. You can do this by re-mortgaging or taking a secured loan. If you are not a homeowner, you will normally have to consider an unsecured consolidation loan. Credit card 0% balance transfers can be a useful little trick as well, as long as you keep on top of your finances and don't borrow any more!

Words of caution

Before going any further into the details of debt consolidation, please carefully consider the following words of caution. First of all, it is vitally important to do a realistic budget-sheet *before* looking into consolidating your debts, understanding that you may have to live on this budget over a period of several years. You should set out a list of your expenses on paper, taking care not to either over-indulge or cut too many corners. You will find the personal budget-sheet at the end of this book ideal for this purpose. When you have worked out your disposable income (i.e. your total income minus reasonable but realistic expenses), that figure should act as the absolute maximum for the monthly repayments that you are aiming for through consolidation. If you find that the repayments you are offered on a consolidation loan are greater than your disposable income figure, consolidation is *not* for you. You would be far wiser to consider bankruptcy or an IVA at this stage. If you enthusiastically consolidate your debts without facing the fact that you are unable to afford even the new monthly payments, sooner or later you will start robbing Peter to pay Paul once again and you will find yourself with more debt that when you started and a gargantuan problem on your hands.

Another pitfall to be aware of is the tendency to successfully consolidate debt, only to fall into further debt through lapsing into a false sense of security. If you manage to consolidate all your debts into a single loan with an affordable minimum monthly repayment, it is tempting to feel that your problems have been solved. At this point, if your credit cards have been cleared, *cut them up*. Also, *close the account* so that you will never again be issued with another card. Otherwise, it is all too easy to put a couple of hundred pounds on credit cards here and there, without feeling that this will make any great difference. But balances can creep up swiftly and insidiously, and before you know it you will be faced with a bigger problem than you had in the first place.

Similarly, even once your debts have been safely consolidated, you need to address the underlying reason that you are in debt in the first place. If this is because of bad money management or an extravagant lifestyle, you must do something to put this right. If these things are not remedied, the problem will only have been temporarily fixed; before too long you will find yourself in a position where your secured loan has been joined by other new debts and the downward spiral will begin all over again.

Finally, it is absolutely vital that you consolidate all of your debts, or at least as many as you possibly can. Leaving debts out of your consolidation arrangement is all too often a recipe for disaster, leading to debts slowly mounting all round. Start off by filling in both a budget-sheet and a list of creditors using the worksheets at the back of this book, and make sure that you consolidate as many of your cards as possible. If you take all of the above advice seriously, you will be able to avoid many of the pitfalls involved in debt consolidation.

Debt Consolidation: the advantages

- Usually you will be given lower monthly payments than before, which can make affordable living possible and enable you to avoid robbing Peter to pay Paul.

- One single monthly payment can make your finances easier to manage.

Debt Consolidation: the disadvantages

- Interest and Payment Protection plans can often prove unreasonably expensive.

- If the consolidation process is not carried out with due care and attention, it will only make the problem worse. For example, if your new monthly payment is still beyond your budget, or if you leave some debts out of the consolidation arrangement, you may soon find more unsecured debts appearing.

Questions and Answers

Q   I am a homeowner. Should I consider releasing equity to consolidate my unsecured debts?

A   If you are a homeowner and there is equity in your property, it is a much better idea to release this equity rather than take more unsecured credit. There are two main reasons for this. Firstly, you will probably be able to borrow more money in this way, thus ensuring that there is no need to leave any debt out of the consolidation process. Unsecured loans are usually capped at around £20000–£25000, whereas secured borrowing is limited only by the sum of equity you are able to release. Secondly, the monthly payment on secured borrowing is always far lower than that of unsecured credit, because secured borrowing has a typical payback period of between 10 and 25 years, whereas unsecured debt has a typical payback period of 5 years. However, don't forget that the mortgage or secured loan is secured on your property; if it is not repaid, you could risk losing your house.

There are two different types of secured consolidation: re-mortgaging or taking out a secured loan. Of these two, re-mortgaging is generally preferable. Because your total payback period will be around 25 years, re-mortgaging usually involves lower monthly costs and lower interest rates. In contrast to this, secured loans usually have a payback period of around 10 years, and interest can be higher, so the monthly payment will be considerably more expensive. It may be easier to take a secured loan, but in my experience it is definitely worth being patient and re-mortgaging so that you can keep your monthly payments as low as possible. Having said that, you may find yourself in a position where it is impossible to re-mortgage. Mortgage providers will normally only be prepared to lend you up to around 85% of the total property value, and if you are already at the limit, you may be unable to extend it. Secured loans, however, can allow you to borrow up to 100% of the equity, and sometimes even up to 110%. If you cannot re-mortgage, then a secured loan might be the best solution. It is worth bearing in mind, however, that secured borrowing is a serious business; whether you are taking a loan or re-mortgaging, the lender has the absolute right to repossess the property if you do not maintain your repayments.

Q Should I enact a credit card balance transfer?

A Balance transfers can often be a very effective way of managing credit card debt. If you have a debt on a credit card, from one point of view it only makes sense to keep transferring the balance onto cards with 0% interest offers, so that you can save on interest payments. However, the key to doing this successfully is to be disciplined and organised with your finances. It is important to read the terms of the credit card agreement carefully, because 0% balances often do not apply when you make a fresh purchase, withdraw cash, miss a monthly payment or use a credit card cheque. The best advice is to make sure you do not use the card! Also, you should make sure that you are aware of the exact date when your 0% period expires, because the credit card company is under no obligation to notify you when this time is up. You should be mindful that a month or two before the end of the 0% period you need to start looking around for a new 0% deal. Finally and most importantly, as mentioned above, the biggest mistake is to allow yourself to relax once your balance is transferred, and feel that you're home and dry – this may not be the case. I have encountered many people over the course of my career who have transferred their balance and felt that all their problems are solved, and in this attitude of complacency begin to spend small amounts here and their on their old credit card. Before you know it, you will end up with two substantial credit card balances rather then one! So be careful not to be lured into a false sense of security. New balances can be run up very quickly and if this happens, your problem will have been made far worse than before. The best advice I can give is to cut up your old credit cards – and cancel the agreements, too, because otherwise you will automatically receive new cards through the post on the renewal dates.

Q   Should I take an unsecured consolidation loan?

A   If you are thinking about taking an unsecured consolidation loan, first you should do a budget-sheet and work out your disposable income figure. Then you should shop around to see if you can find a loan that gives you monthly repayments that fit within that amount. If you find such a loan, that is certainly very promising; however, before signing on the dotted line there are still more investigations to be made. A common mistake is to simply look at the monthly amount, see if it is affordable, sign the Agreement and take the money – without taking the time to consider how much will be paid in total, including all the interest and payment protection charges.

It is easy to get bamboozled by APR, interest rates and charges. But don't despair – it does not need to be that complicated. A quick and simple way to find out the total cost of a consolidation loan, including interest and charges, is to take the monthly repayment figure and multiply it by the number of payments you will need to make. For example, if you owe £8000 to multiple creditors, and the creditors are asking for £500 per month between them, you may decide to take out a consolidation loan of £8,000 at a monthly rate of only £190. This new loan may demand 60 monthly payments over a period of 5 years. On the face of it, this seems very good, because your monthly payments have been halved. However, in reality your total payback figure will be £11400 (60 x £190). Thus you will end up paying back £3400 in interest and charges alone. Before you took out the consolidation loan, you only owed £8000 – so even though your monthly payment has reduced, you've taken on a further debt of £3400! This example illustrates the importance of considering your loan deal carefully before proceeding, without simply jumping at the chance to reduce your monthly payments.

Q Should I sign up for Payment Protection Plan?

A Here's a little secret that the creditors don't want you to know: more often than not, Payment Protection is money for old rope. If you are interested in getting debt-free as soon as possible, there are better alternatives to Payment Protection. There are various reasons why taking Payment Protection must be considered very carefully. Payment Protection will only cover you for the one single loan, and often only for one single year of unemployment. Furthermore, it will only pay out if you have explicitly been made redundant, and this point is carefully checked. If you have left the job of your own accord, even if the company goes bust shortly afterwards, you may not receive a penny from Payment Protection. This is especially relevant to self-employed people, who cannot by definition be made redundant; for these people, Payment Protection will very rarely pay out, and signing up is often a total waste of money. To make matters worse, your Payment Protection fees are put on top of your total loan before interest is added. This means that not only are you paying into a Payment Protection policy that will probably never pay out, you are paying interest on it as well!

As an alternative to Payment Protection, there are many excellent Income Protection policies available that are far better and less expensive. My advice would be to find a good Independent Financial Advisor. Through their services you should be able to get an insurance policy that a) offers genuine cover for your *entire income*, whether you are self-employed or not, b) will pay out for an *extended* period of unavoidable unemployment, and c) charges are not much greater than you would otherwise pay in Payment Protection, and the cover provided is many times more comprehensive and effective.

Summary

Consolidating debts can be a tricky business. It will only work if you proceed with caution, armed with enough knowledge to allow you to distinguish good consolidation offers from bad ones. Here are the main points to be aware of:

1 Complete a realistic budget-sheet first. Only proceed with consolidation if the monthly payments fit within your disposable income figure.

2 Make sure that you consolidate all your debts, or as many as possible.

3 If your debts were accumulated as a result of bad money-management, ensure that you make every effort to overcome these tendencies.

4 If your consolidation is successful, be wary of falling into a false sense of security and borrowing more money. On no account use your old credit cards again, or take new ones.

5 Consider all the options very carefully before deciding to sign up for Payment Protection. If you are would like an alternative, take Income Protection Insurance through a reputable Independent Financial Advisor.

6 Before signing on the dotted line for a loan, work out how much you are going to pay in total – including interest – by multiplying your monthly payment by the payback period. Only go ahead if this payback seems reasonable to you.

What to do next?

If you are interested in consolidating your debts, make sure that you take into account the advice above. Your first step should be to fill out the budget-sheet at the back of this book, so that you are absolutely clear how much you can afford to pay in monthly payments. Then you should shop around a range of different lenders, either by searching online or visiting High Street banks and building societies. Before agreeing to a loan, make sure that you are aware of the total amount you are going to pay back, you have carefully considered the option of Payment Protection, and that the repayments fall within your disposable income. By following the guidelines in this chapter and judging your loan offers by these criteria, you should be able to avoid unfair deals and come to a good arrangement that is sustainable in the long term.

Case Study

Pauline Hutchings began her professional career working for a large Horticultural Centre in East Anglia. She worked there for almost ten years, and during that time her salary climbed from £10000 per year to £18000. However, after ten years of work she wanted to make the move from being an employee to being self-employed; she felt that a self-employed lifestyle would allow her greater freedom and independence, and hopefully bring back more money as well.

She decided to use her professional horticultural experience and start up a landscape gardening business. Since she knew the market already, she was confident that the business would be successful; however, she didn't have any capital to buy a van and gardening equipment. She decided to use credit cards to fund these purchases, and because of her clean credit rating was able to immediately receive cards with hefty limits. First of all she borrowed £5000 from one card and used that money to buy equipment, and then she borrowed a further £5000 from a second card to fund the purchase of a van.

However, the business did not do as well as Pauline had initially hoped. It took her three months before she began to break even, and in that time she turned to a third credit card for her living expenses. This left her with a total debt of £13000, spread across three cards. She found that when business was good, the repayments were not a problem. However, her average earnings were too low and she soon found herself robbing Peter to pay Paul in order to meet her monthly repayments. In this way she ran up a further £2000, bringing her total debt to £15000 with monthly bills of £450. She realised that something had to be done.

Pauline did not want to go bankrupt because she was wary of the stigma attached to it. She looked on the Internet and contacted Thomas Charles & Co Ltd with a view to proposing an IVA. However, a Debt Advisor analysed her financial affairs and felt that her situation could be better solved with a sensible consolidation loan. Because she was usually disciplined with her money and these debts were taken for a specific purpose, the Debt Advisor believed that if Pauline were to take a consolidation loan that reduced her monthly payments, she would be successful in maintaining her payments and living within her budget. The Debt Advisor also provided her with a budget-sheet that she could use to get her finances clear in her head before approaching the lenders.

Pauline went online and found that HSBC could offer her a consolidation loan of £15000. This gave her a monthly payment of only £295, which fell comfortably within the disposable income on her budget-sheet. She calculated that she would end up paying back a total of £18900 over a period of 6 years. She refused payment protection, which she calculated would add a further £1400 onto her total debt! Even so, she would be required to pay over £3900 in interest. However, she came to the decision that it was worth paying this amount in return for reducing her monthly payments to fit within her budget. She successfully applied for this loan and immediately regained control of her finances. Now her business is picking up, and she is thinking of expanding. She considers her money crisis as just a blip, and she is well on the way to financial security.

Chapter Five

Rags To Riches: Managing Your Money

If you want to solve your debt problem for good, there are two things that need to be done. Firstly you should do some research and decide which of the four debt solutions described in this book is best for you, and take the necessary steps to put it in place. Secondly, you should evaluate your monthly spending and take control of your financial lifestyle. This second point is absolutely vital because if you fail to take a long, hard look at your budgeting habits, you may run the risk of self-sabotaging whatever solution you are seeking to put in place. On the other hand, if you *do* improve your budgeting, your debt solution will be supported by good money management and before too long you will be well on the way to debt freedom.

For ease of memory, I have structured the 4 essential points of advice around the acronym 'RICH':

R ealise what your budget is

I magine your available budget in your head

C heck your budget as you spend

H elp yourself to future security

1. Realise what your budget is

The very first step on the journey from rags to riches is to have a clear-headed look at your monthly spending. In my experience, most people are actually unaware of their various monthly expenses (and this is often especially true of those who have found themselves in serious debt). For example, most car owners spend an average of £35–£45 on car maintenance each month. This figure might seem quite high, but only if you make the mistake of thinking in the short-term rather than the long-term. If you take a long-term view and factor in the annual services, MOT tests and occasional repairs, that would easily come to around £500 a year – which averages at £41.66 per month – an expense you may be unaware of. Thus if you fail to allocate a realistic car maintenance budget each month, when the time comes to pay these bills you will find yourself invariably turning to your credit card.

Similarly, smoking is an expense that is often ignored. If you smoke ten cigarettes a day and a packet costs £5, your smoking bill will come to £75.77 each month. In addition to this there are often bills associated with pets, contact lenses and insurance policies which are often overlooked. On top of these expenses it is prudent to allow yourself at least £30–£50 per month as 'emergency money'.

It is tempting to be over-optimistic when estimating simple expenses such as clothing. In my experience I have found that the average UK adult who is making an effort to live prudently spends at least £50 per month on clothing alone. This may seem reasonable, or even on the slim side, to the average person on the street. However, people with debt problems are accustomed to living on a shoestring, and often feel that £50 a month on clothes is a large amount of money. I have even encountered people who claim to spend nothing on clothing at all! This confusion is again due to a failure to take the long-term view. It may be the case that no money is being spent on clothes at this present time, but things will not remain that way indefinitely. Sooner or later clothes must be bought, and these expenses should be taken into account and budgeted for in the form of a monthly allowance. The way to arrive at reliable budget figures is to fill in the budget-sheet at the back of this book carefully and realistically. This will give you a clear idea of exactly how much money you can spend on each individual expense, and you will have a basis for good money management.

2. Imagine your available budget in your head

The second step is to subtract your fixed living expenses (usually everything apart from food, clothes and miscellaneous expenditure) from your monthly income and make a note of the amount you have left. This new figure is your available budget. For example, if you bring home £1200 each month, once you take away fixed expenses such as rent, council tax, transport expenses, phone bills and so on, the available budget figure may actually be closer to £350. It is important to have this £350 figure clear in your mind because if the budget that you have in your head is greater than the money in your account, you will be liable to withdraw too much when you go to the cash-point. It is even worth trying to forget the £1200 altogether, and just focus on your £350 available budget. This will ensure that your spending does not stray over the boundaries of your budget, and ensure that there is always enough to cover direct debt payments coming out of your account. So you should imagine your available budget in your head as clearly as you can.

3. Check your budget as you spend

The third step is to ensure that you stick to the budget that you have worked out. This is an absolutely vital part of any rags-to-riches journey. The first two steps so far have been largely hypothetical; the challenge now is to take your budget into your everyday life and use it to keep on top of your spending. The best way of doing this, particularly when you are getting used to a new lifestyle, is to keep a detailed record of what you spend. It is good to have a small notebook that you can carry around with you. At the top of the first page, write the amount of money you will bring home that month. Below this write a list of your fixed living expenses, including all direct debts and standing orders, and at the bottom of the page write your available budget. Highlight this figure – it is the one you are going to imagine in your head. From then on, you can list everything you spend as you go. It is best to keep this record in as much detail as possible, so that you can check exactly how much money you have spent on your various different expenses at any time. Of course I am not suggesting that you get your notebook out every time you are at the till in the supermarket, but at least update it when you have a spare moment. This will mean that you are able to check your budgeting whenever you like, and adjust your spending if need be to ensure that you are sticking to your available budget. It also means that if your budget does not add up at the end of the month, you can look back over your spending and pinpoint the problem.

It is important to recognise that no one is saying this is going to be easy. It entails living within a strict budget, and this may mean not buying that new clothing item or video game if it outside your available budget. However, if you develop the habit of being disciplined, you will soon be able to reap the rewards.

4. Help yourself to future security

Once you have the first three steps in place, you should be well on the way to efficient day-to-day money management. The final step is to make sure that you do not backslide into debt in the future as a result of a sudden, unforeseen expense. For example, if you should suddenly encounter a redundancy, a death in the family or a period of sickness, you will not have the money to guarantee security at that time. So if you want to avoid falling back into debt, you need to start planning your future security now.

The way to do this is simple: learn to save. First review your available budget in the ways mentioned above and establish a figure that you feel you can comfortably spare from it each month to put aside for the future. The next thing you need to do is get this money squirreled away as quickly and smoothly as possible; as the old adage goes, 'out of sight, out of mind'. You should open a high-interest savings account, and set a direct debit coming from your main account into your savings account every month. Ensure this happens as soon as you are paid. If you wait until the end of the month it will be too late, and your planned saving money will be spent! You should subtract your savings contribution from your budget so that your available budget figure once again reflects the amount of money that is available to spend. Then you should visualise that new figure in your head, and check your spending so that it stays within your available budget. Then you should forget all about your savings contributions. If you are aware in the back of your mind that you have a spare amount of money that you are choosing to contribute towards savings, there will be a strong temptation to dip into that money, and before you know it your savings plan will start to dwindle. Therefore, if you forget all about your savings account, there is every hope that you will gradually accumulate a financial cushion that will help you towards financial security in the future.

The same principle can be applied to dealing with overdraft debts. If you still have an overdraft once you have put your debt solution in place, one effective way to pay it off is to assign it a monthly contribution from your budget. In this way you will be relating to an available budget that factors in an overdraft contribution, and you will automatically be taking steps each month to clear it.

In conclusion, then, these four basic steps can greatly help you to manage your money efficiently and make sure that your debt solution is given the very best chance of success.

Tackling addiction

One final point to bear in mind is that your debt problem may be stemming from an underlying emotional issue. This is something you should think seriously about, and if you believe that you may be a compulsive debtor, you should seek professional help. Telltale signs of being a compulsive debtor are:

- An attitude that 'lives for the present' and is unconcerned about the future.

- Feelings of inhibition or embarrassment when money comes up in conversation.

- Being unaware of your financial situation such as income, expenditure and debts.

- Frequently buying things and returning them; never using items once they have been bought; impulse buying.

- Finding it difficult to fulfil your responsibilities, and feeling a disproportionate sense of achievement when you manage to do so.

- Always having a financial crisis to contend with, such as bouncing cheques, robbing Peter to pay Paul, or borrowing money in the hope that funds will somehow appear.

- An unfounded sense that someone will bail you out if things get serious.

- Getting a buzz from paying for things on credit – a sensation of being part of an exclusive club or that you are living an adult lifestyle.

- Borrowing small, insignificant items from friends and never giving them back.

- Self-punishment; denying your own basic needs in order to pay your creditors.

If these symptoms sound familiar to you, I would recommend that you make every effort to solve this problem through seeking professional help. One option is to consider 'Debtors Anonymous', which operates a '12-step programme' based on Alcoholics Anonymous.

Appendices

BUDGET-SHEET

Total Net monthly income:	
Rent payments / Mortgage contributions	
Monthly 2nd Mortgage / other secured borrowings	
Garage rent / fixed service charge on property	
Council tax	
Water rates	
House & Contents insurance	
Life insurance & Critical illness Insurance	
Pension	
Mortgage protection insurance	
Endowment Contributions	
Electricity / Gas	
Wood / Coal / Oil etc	
Food	
Cosmetics, cleaning products, household items	
Entertainments	
Clothing	
Optician's bills	
Haircuts	
Child maintenance (through Child Support Agency or private arrangement)	
Telephone	
Household appliance rental	
TV licence	
Travelling (public transport)	
Car petrol	
Car insurance	
Car road tax	
Car maintenance	
Car hire purchase	
Other hire purchase	
School / Nursery: Fees, Meals, Travel	
Child minding	
Medical	
Pet expenses / smoking	
County Court Judgements	
Emergency money	
Other (please specify)	
TOTAL EXPENDITURE	

Note: All figures should be inclusive of interest and charges.

	Name of Creditor	Loan/Card	Debt in Name of:	Amount Outstanding	Monthly Payment (£)	Notes
1						
2						
3						
4						
5						
6						
7						
8						
9						
10						
11						
12						
13						
14						
15						
16						
17						
18						
TOTAL:						

Useful Statistics

Personal Insolvency Statistics

- 45% increase in PIs in England and Wales in 2005

- PIs increased by 15% in the 4th quarter 2005

- PIs saw a 57% increase since the 4th Q 2004

- The total of PI has doubled in the last 3 years

- 3 million people faced Christmas 2005 with over £10,000 debts

- In London 1 in 10 have debts over £10,000 excluding mortgages

- There were 20,461 PIs in England and Wales in the fourth quarter of 2005, 15% more than the previous 3 months, which at the time were the highest figure since records began

- PI has seen a 15.0% increase from the 3rd quarter 2005 and an increase of 57.1% from the same period in2004.

- An estimated 200,000 people will face PI in 2006

- 12,000 people were insolvent in the 3rd quarter of 2005

- 67,580 people became insolvent in 2005

- 13,020 people became insolvent in 2004

- Insolvencies are up 45% since 2004

- 5% of adults say the often spend more than they earn

- Average household income is £25,000/year

- The average debt of those forced into insolvency is more than £37, 000 on cards and personal loans

- PI (including bankruptcies) has risen to £60,000/year

- 250,000 people are signed up for debt management plans

- 1.5million people who are on the verge of insolvency can only make the minimum payments

- 65% of defaults on debt repayments are made by 25–35yr olds

- The above has gone up 15% since 2003

IVA Statistics

- IVAs have doubled in the past 2 years to 20,293

- In the 4th Q 2005 there was 6,960 IVAs

- There was an increase of 23.9% from the 3rd to the 4th quarter 2005

- There was an increase of 117.1% from the 4th quarter 2005 to the corresponding quarter of the 2004

- In 2005 IVAs saw a 95% increase from the 3rd Q compared to the 3rd Quarter in 2004

- Since 1998 IVAs have helped more than 50 000 people out of debt

- IVAs made up of 30% of total insolvencies in 2005

Bankruptcy Statistics

- 203,000 were on the verge of declaring themselves bankrupt in 2005

- 13,501 bankruptcies in the 4th Q 2005

- An increase of 10.9% from the 3rd to 4th quarter 2005

- An increase of 37.6% on the 4th quarter 2005 since corresponding quarter of 2004,

- 16% of bankruptcies are caused by business failure (John Tribe Report)

- 35% are caused by bad relationships, redundancy or illness (John Tribe Report)

- The number of houses affected by bankruptcy has gone from one in every 1000, three years ago, to 3 in every 1000.

Home Repossessions / Mortgage Statistics

- The number of people 3–6 months behind on their mortgage payments were 21% higher than the end of 2004 when it was at (32,470)

- People more than 12months behind in arrears rose by 23% to 13,820 since 2004

- Between Oct- Dec 2005 court orders to repossess homes were up by 58% from the same period 2004

- 10,260 properties were repossessed during 2005,

- 70% more homes were repossessed in 2005 than 2004, however this is the 3rd lowest figure since 1983

- HRs are expected to reach 120,000 in both 2006 and 2007

- Half of home repossessions granted by court result in eviction

- 1,400 householders were evicted in 2005

- Brighton is the highest on the home repossession list for 4th Q 2005

Consumer debt and over-spending Statistics

- Overspending is estimated at £8.1billion/year

- In December 2005 47% of consumers had unsecured borrowing of £10,000 or more.

- The average household owes £7,650, not including mortgages

- Britons owe £1.13trillion (That is £1,130000000000.00)

- The above is equivalent to the combined gross domestic product of the worlds 155 least wealthy nations

- Mortgage debt for houses accounts for 80% of the 1.13trillion national debt

- In Nov 2005 consumer debt rose by £927m, which is the smallest increase in 5 years

- Rising 10% every year

Credit / Store Cards Statistics

- 74million credit cards have been issued in Britain

- 55.3% of all credit cards in Europe belong to Britons

- The UK haves 5 times the European average amount of credit cards

- By 2009 credit card possessions are estimated to rise to 99.2million cards

- 90% of credit card companies fail to check the income of applicants

Corporate Debt Statistics

- There were 3187 company liquidations in the 4th quarter 2005

- Company Liquidations are up 8,5% since 2004

- Company L are down 5.5% from 3rd to 4th quarter 2005

Financial Institution Statistics

- Estimate an 11% rise in after-tax earnings for 2006

- Banks wrote off 3.6 billion in unsecured loans during 2005

- A £1000 Barclay card debt will take 25yrs to pay off if making minimum repayment.

Statistics Acknowledgements

- The facts on our statistics pages are taken from the following sources:
- The Financial Times
- The Independent
- The Economist
- The Daily Telegraph
- The Times
- The Guardian
- The Sunday Telegraph
- Reuters News
- The Evening Standard
- The Daily Mail
- The Daily Mirror
- The Sunday Mirror
- The Guardian Unlimited
- The Mail on Sunday
- Dow Jones International News
- The Western Mail
- The Birmingham Post
- PA Newswire
- PR Newswire Europe
- The Express on Sunday
- The Scotsman

- Comtex News Network

- Lancashire Evening Post

- The Sentinel

- Scottish Daily Record & Sunday Mail

- Manchester Evening News

- Coventry Evening Telegraph

- The Gazette

- BBC News Online

- The Birmingham Mail

- The Journal

Glossary of Terms

A

Abandonment

The voluntary relinquishment of ownership by failure to use the property, coupled with intent to abandon.

Add on Interest

Add on interest is a method of charging interest. Interest is computed on the total amount borrowed and added on to the principal. Each payment is then deducted from this total amount. Interest on real estate loans is usually figured based on the balance owing after each payment is made.

Amortization

Amortization is payments of debt in equal instalments of principal and interest, rather than interest only payments.

Annual Percentage Rate (APR)

The yearly interest percentage of a loan, as expressed by the actual rate of interest paid. For example: 6% add-on interest would be much more than 6% simple interest, even though both would say 6%. The A.P.R. is disclosed as a requirement of federal truth in lending statutes and should include all finance charges.

Arrears

A payment made after it is due is in arrears. Interest is said to be paid in arrears since it is paid to the date of payment rather than in advance, as is rent.

Arrestment

This means that money or goods held by a third party are 'frozen'. The most common example is arrestment of funds in your bank account. The third party (eg a bank) may agree to hand the property (funds) over to a creditor.

Asset

An asset is property that belongs to an individual. Including; real property (land or buildings) and personal property (eg cash, stocks and shares, or vehicles).

Attachment

This means that goods held by the person in debt, eg a car, are 'frozen'. Anything that has been frozen ('attached') can be sold. The money raised is then handed over to the person who is owed the money.

Average life

The length of time that will pass before one-half of a debt obligation has been retired.

B

Balance

The amount of money in an account, equal to the net of credits and debits at that point in time for that account is a balance.

Bankruptcy

A form of debt relief. There are two kinds of bankruptcy:

Personal bankruptcy;

An individual, sole trader or partnership is formally declared bankrupt by the court (ie they cannot pay their debts) and that the debts and assets of a person should transfer to an appointed trustee.

Company bankruptcy;

Companies can also fail and if this happens, the company is said to be insolvent. It may be made subject to liquidation, receivership or an administration order issued by the courts.

Beneficial Loan

A loan made by an employer to an employee on which interest is either not charged or is less than the official rate. The difference between the interest charged and the official rate is taxable.

Beneficiary

The Person who is entitled to receive funds of property under the terms and provisions of a will, trust, insurance policy or security instrument. In connection with a mortgage loan the beneficiary is the lender.

Benefits

Benefits are paid to you by the state and include income support, child benefit, job seeker's allowance, disability benefit, housing benefit, and council tax benefit.

Binding

For example, an agreement, which is binding cannot be legally avoided or stopped.

Budget

A list of all your income and expenditure is a budget.

Budget deficit

A deficit is the gap between spending and revenue and thus the amount that may need to be borrowed.

Building Society

'Mutual' non-profit-making institutions set up to lend money to their members for house purchase. Building societies are 'mutual;' because they are owned by their members, and their members are entitled to their profits and benefits.

C

Cap rate

The discount rate used to determine the present value of a stream of future earnings. Typically this will be an appropriate risk-free return plus a premium to reflect the risk of that specific investment.

Cash

This is currency and coins on hand, bank balances, and negotiable money orders and checks.

Ceiling

The maximum interest rate permitted by state law for a given loan. A ceiling is a common feature of floating rate notes. An upper limit on the exchange rate of a country's currency imposed by some regulatory authorities (the government or regulators will step in and ensure that the exchange rate does not exceed the ceiling).

CEO (Chief Executive Officer)

Is the executive who is responsible for a company's operations, usually the President or the Chairman of the Board.

Citizens Advice Bureau

An office represented in most towns in the UK, where the public can obtain free advice on an extensive range of civil matters including social security, consumer matters such as loans and rental arrears, employment, housing matters such as mortgage and rent arrears, legal matters such as legal aid, family matters, taxation and many other subjects.

Classified Property Tax

Property tax which varies in rate depending on the use of the property.

Credit

Credit is an agreement in which a borrower receives something of value now and agrees to repay the lender later.

Creditor

A creditor is an individual or a company that is owed money by another person.

Currency

Any form of money that is in public circulation. \D

DAS administrator

The Accountant in Bankruptcy is the DAS administrator. They are responsible for maintaining the DAS Register which contains details of debt payment programs (DPPs), and for the approval of money advisers, payments distributors and debt payment programs (DPPs).

DAS approved money adviser

A DAS approved money adviser is a general money adviser who has received further training (and been approved by the DAS administrator) to act on behalf of the debtor to negotiate a debt payment program (DPP) under DAS.

Death Benefit

The payment made to a beneficiary from an annuity or policy when the policyholder dies.

Debt

Any money that is owed or due to someone else.

Debt Capital

Debt Capital is the capital raised through the issuance of bonds.

Debt consolidation

Debt consolidation is the replacement of multiple loans with a single loan, often with a lower monthly payment and a longer repayment period. It can also be called a consolidation loan.

Debt-equity swap

Debt equity swap is a transaction in which existing bonds (debt) are exchanged for newly issued stock (equity). For example, an individual can in essence cancel a portion of their debt and transfer the equivalent balance to equity. A debt-equity swap can help an individual that is in financial trouble by cancelling some of their outstanding debt.

Debt management

A form of dealing with debt where the debtor can pay their debts (including interest and penalty charges) in full - they just need a bit more time. The debtor will keep control of their assets and most importantly they will keep their home.

Debt payment program (DPP)

An agreement under the Debt Arrangement Scheme (DAS) that allows you to pay off your debts over an extended period of time. The program can be for any amount of money or for any reasonable length of time.

Debt relief

The last resort for a debtor when dealing with debt where the debtor cannot pay their debts - bankruptcy. The debtor will lose control of their assets, possibly including their home and their credit rating will be greatly affected.

Debtor

A debtor is an individual or sole trader who owes money to another person or company (creditor).

Deduction

An expense subtracted from adjusted gross income when calculating taxable income, such as for state and local taxes paid, charitable gifts, and certain types of interest payments.

Default Notice

This is a letter reminding a debtor that they haven't paid their debt. This must be issued by a creditor in respect of debts covered by the Consumer Credit Act 1974 before any further action is taken.

Demand

The lender's statement of the amount due to pay of a loan.

Diligence

We all rely on people keeping their promises. If a promise is not kept the courts may order someone to pay what they are due.

There are a number of ways that people can be made to pay after a court order has been made. The most common forms of court enforcement, or diligence, are arrestment, earnings arrestment and attachment. There are other less common ways to enforce court orders. They include inhibition and adjudication, and your lawyer or adviser can tell you more about them if needed.

Diligence Stopper

A court order which stops the operation of existing diligence and prevents future diligence.

Direct debit

An instruction you give to your bank or building society to make regular payments from your account to a specific company. Unlike a standing order you agree that the creditor can vary this amount each month.

Disclaimer

A statement made to free oneself from responsibility.

Discounted Loan

A loan on which the interest and financing charges are deducted from the face amount when the loan is issued.

E

Earnings

Revenues minus expenses and taxes. Also called income.

Earnings Arrestment

If you are working, the money you owe to a creditor can be taken from your wages/salary directly from your employer by an earnings arrestment.

Endowment

A permanent fund bestowed upon an individual or institution, such as a university, museum, hospital, or foundation, to be used for a specific purpose.

Entitlement

Benefits guaranteed to an individual, such as dividends for shareholders or government aid for those who qualify.

Equity

The value of a person's interest in real property after all liens and charges have been deducted.

F

Fee

A charge for services rendered.

Final Salary

The basis of determining a person's pension entitlement in a final salary scheme and which normally refers to an occupational pension.

Finance

Finance deals with matters related to money and the markets.

Flexible Mortgage Account

A combined mortgage and current account. Any savings each month earn the mortgage rate, which is a relatively high and tax-free rate of return.

Frozen Account

A bank account whose funds may not be withdrawn until a lien is satisfied or an ownership dispute is resolved.

Funds

A pool of money normally set apart for a purpose, for example, a pension fund to provide pensions.

G

Gold Card

A plastic payment card which normally allows the holder higher spending limits over the standard card. Also loan facilities are sometimes available. People who hold such a card are often required to be earning a minimum salary level. Gold cards are usually either charge cards or credit cards.

Grace Period

The period, normally 30 days, during which an insurance policy remains in force even though the premium has not been paid.

Grant

Funding for a non-profit organization, usually for a specific project.

Grantee

One to whom a grant is made.

Gross Income

The scheduled (total) income, either actual or estimated, of a person before deductions. This for example could be a person's salary plus bonuses, plus benefits in kind (e.g. company car and medical insurance) plus income from shares etc.

Growing Equity Mortgage (GEM)

A fixed rate, graduated payment loan allowing low beginning payments and a shorter term because of higher payments as the loan progress. This is based on the theory of increasing income by the buyer and, therefore ability to make higher future payments.

Guarantee

A commitment made by a person to be answerable for the debts or liabilities of another.

H

Hidden asset

Asset not immediately apparent from a balance sheet.

High equity

A mortgage which is low in comparison to the amount deposited in cash by the purchaser.

Hire purchase (HP)

The pre-agreed purchase of an asset where the asset e.g. computer is in your possession as long as repayments are kept to. Once enough payments are made, the asset becomes your property.

Holder

A person in possession of a negotiable instrument such as a bill of exchange or promissory note. That person may be the payee or the endorsee, or a person who has made an opening purchase of an option and thus has acquired the rights to them.

I

Incapacity Benefit

A state benefit payable after the expiry of state sickness benefit if a person is still unfit to work. This replaces the former invalidity benefit and as such carries a reduced level of benefit.

Income

Money received by an individual as a salary, or from investments. Cash deposits and bonds will provide income in the form of interest. This income is subject to income tax.

Income from property

Income received from property letting is subject to income tax. The amount taxable is the amount receivable in the tax year. If an owner, occupier or tenant rents out a room he may receive up to a certain annual income without incurring a tax liability.

Income tax

In most countries income tax is progressive on successive slices of income, so that the more you earn the higher the incremental rates of tax you pay.

In the UK, everyone is allowed to make a certain amount of income before any tax is payable. Known as the 'personal allowance', the amount increases with age, and for the year 2005-2006 the figures are:

> Under 65: £4,895
> 65–74: £7,090
> 75 and over: £7,220

If your income in a tax year is below these thresholds, you are not liable for income tax. In some circumstances, where tax has been deducted at source, you will be able to reclaim tax already paid.

For earnings above your personal allowance, your income tax liability will go up in bands and vary according to whether the income is from employment, share dividends or interest. The lowest rate is 10% and the highest is 40%.Inflation The overall general upward price movement of goods and services in an economy. Over time, as the cost of goods and services increase, the value of the pound is going to fall because a person won't be able to purchase as much with that pound as he/she previously could.

Inland Revenue

The government department responsible to the Treasury for the collection of direct taxes which include income tax, capital gains tax and inheritance tax etc.

Insolvent

Unable to meet debt obligations.

Instalment

The regular periodic payment that a borrower agrees to make to a lender.

Insured Mortgage

A mortgage insured against loss to the mortgagee in the event of default and a failure of the mortgaged property to satisfy the balance owing plus costs of foreclosure.

Interest

The fee charged by a lender to a borrower for the use of borrowed money, usually expressed as an annual percentage of the principal; the rate is dependent upon the time value of money, the credit risk of the borrower, and the inflation rate. Here, interest per year divided by principal amount, expressed as a percentage (also called interest rate).

Interest Cap

The maximum interest rate increase of an Adjustable Mortgage Loan. For example: a 120% loan with a 5% interest rate cap would have maximum interest for the life of the loan which would not exceed 17%.

Interest Rate

The percentage rate at which interest is charged on a loan or paid on savings etc.

J

Joint

Pertaining to multiple parties on the same side of an agreement or transaction.

Joint account

Typically a bank or brokerage account in the names of two (or more) people. Arrangements can be made such that either individual or all signatures are required when drawing checks/cheques.

Joint liability

The legal liability of two or more people for claims against or debts incurred by them jointly. If three people have joint liability and are indebted to another party, they may only be sued as a group and not individually.

L

Late charge

A charge imposed by a lender to a borrower when the borrower fails to make payment on the due date.

Laundering

The manipulation of money obtained in a wrongful manner, for example theft, so as to seem to have originated from a lawful source. An example is to pay the unlawful money into an overseas bank and subsequently transfer back to the country of origin.

Lease

A contract in which the legal owner of property or other asset agrees to another person using that property or asset in return for a regular specified payment (known as rent) over a set term. In addition to buildings, other items such as cars and computers are often leased in order to avoid capital costs in the running of a business.

Legacy

Another term for bequest, that is, the making of a gift by will. In the main there are three main types of legacy.

Pecuniary legacy: A gift of a fixed sum of money left for example to an individual or a charity.

Specific legacy: A gift of a specific item (such as a set of books) left for example to a friend.

Residuary legacy: A gift consisting of the residue of an estate after all other conditions of the will have been met, or part of such residue.

Lender

A person or company that offers to lend money to a borrower for a given period of time. The borrower is obliged to repay the loan either by instalments or single payment together with specified interest.

Liability

The debts of a person or company.

Liability Insurance

Insurance against legal liability to pay compensation and court costs where the insured has been found negligent in respect of injuries sustained by another person or damage to his/her property.

Life assurance

An insurance policy which, in return for the payment of regular premiums, pays a lump sum on the death of the insured. In the case of policies limited to investments which have a cash value, in addition to life cover, a savings element provides benefits which are payable before death. In the UK endowment assurance provides life cover or a maturity value after a specified term, whichever is the sooner.

Liquid Assets

Cash plus assets which can readily be converted into cash.

Liquidated Damages

A definite amount of damages, set forth in a contract, to be paid by the party breaching the contract. A pre-determined estimate of actual damages from a breach.

Loan

An advance of money from a lender to a borrower over a period of time. The borrower is obliged to repay the loan either at intervals during or at the end of the loan period together with interest.

Loan Account

An account, opened for a customer by a bank, following the granting of a loan. The amount of the loan is credited to the customer's current account and similarly debited to the loan account. An arrangement is subsequently made for the customer to repay the loan, usually over a stated period of time, with interest additionally being paid on the outstanding amount.

Loan Policy

A title insurance policy insuring a mortgagee, or beneficiary under a deed of trust, against loss caused by invalid title in the borrower, or loss caused by invalid title in the borrower, or loss of priority of the mortgage or deed of trust.

Loan ratio

The ratio, expressed as a percentage, of the amount of a loan to the value or selling price of real property. Usually, the higher the percentage, the greater the interest charged. Maximum percentages for banks, savings and loans, or government insured loans, is set by statute.

Loan Sharking

Charging an illegally high interest rate on a loan.

Lower earnings limit

The level of income at which employees start to pay Class 1 National Insurance contributions.

Limited (LTD)

'Ltd' after a company name indicates that the company is privately owned with 'limited liability' status. This means that the directors of the company are not liable for the company's debts if it goes bust. Nearly all newly-formed companies in the UK are incorporated as Ltd companies. If the number of shareholders in the company grows to 50 or more, the company changes to a 'plc' – public limited company, though this does not mean that their shares are publicly tradable. Only companies that formally list their shares on the Stock Exchange are fully tradable.

Lump Sum

A sum of money paid in a single instalment.

M

Maximizing income

Increasing the amount of income you earn.

Money adviser

Someone who is trained to offer advice both on debt and on increasing your income. A money adviser can help you work out what your options are and, where needed, negotiate affordable payments and set up repayment plans with your creditors.

Money Broker

A type of agent who arranges short term loans between banks (which are seeking to lend money) and borrowers such as institutions. The money broker is not involved in the process of lending/borrowing but merely acts as an intermediary earning a commission.

Mortgage

A loan in which the borrower (the mortgagor) offers a property and land as security to the lender (the mortgagee) until the loan is repaid. Repayments of the loan are usually made on a monthly basis over a long period of time, typically 25 years. In the UK, the most common forms of mortgage are the repayment mortgage and the interest only mortgage.

Mortgage Broker

A person or company engaged in the arrangement of mortgages for buyers. The broker is usually paid a commission by the lender.

Mortgage Protection

Term assurance to cover the repayment of a mortgage in the event of the death of the mortgagor during the period of the loan. In the case of a repayment mortgage the capital sum outstanding is gradually reduced over the term of the loan (albeit slowly during the initial years when the majority of the repayments are paying the interest) so that decreasing term assurance would be incorporated in the policy. For an endowment mortgage where the sum assured and the death benefit are at least equal to the amount of the loan throughout the term of the loan, level term assurance would be apt.

N

National Debt

The total debt accumulated by a government through the issue of government bonds, Treasury bills and Treasury notes. The government has to pay interest on its borrowings, and this obligation is one of the major budget items for many governments.

National Insurance

A form of taxation, payable by employees, employers and the self employed, which is notionally to fund state benefits including pensions, sickness, unemployment and maternity. It is part of the state's social security system and ultimately controlled by the Department of Social Security.

Negative equity

A situation where the purchaser of a property has taken out a mortgage and some time after the purchase, the value of the property falls below the mortgage amount.

Negotiable

The ability to be sold or transferred to another party as a form of payment. Something which is negotiable is transferable by endorsement and delivery. A negotiable instrument could be a check made out to you, because you could endorse it for payment to you or transfer it to someone else as payment to them.

Net / After deductions

An amount of money e.g. income you take home after income tax, national insurance contributions, payments towards a pension scheme or any other deductions have been deducted, usually by your employer when you get paid.

Net assets

Total assets minus total liabilities of an individual or company.

Net Income

Net profit attributable to ordinary shareholders after the deduction of all other charges.

Nominee

The person, bank or brokerage in whose name securities are transferred.

Notarization

The certification by a Notary Public that a person signing a document has been properly identified. Notarization does not certify the content of a document, only validity of signature.

Notary Public

A person authorized to notarize certain documents.

O

Obligation bond

Mortgage bond whose face value exceeds the value of the underlying property, and for which a personal obligation is created to compensate the lender for any costs that may exceed the value of the mortgage.

Ombudsman

Ombudsmen do not have any formal power to reverse decisions but they have substantial moral authority over companies or national or local government agencies.

Within financial services, there are different Ombudsmen for banking, building societies, insurance, pensions, and investments.

If you have a complaint about your treatment by a financial services company, the first thing you should do is make the complaint directly to the compliance officer or senior management of the company. If the outcome is unsatisfactory, you can then take it to the Ombudsman who will investigate and consider all the facts of the case, and make a recommendation. The company will not always follow the Ombudsman's recommendation, but usually will.

Open-end mortgage

A mortgage permitting the mortgagor to borrow additional money under the same mortgage, with certain conditions, usually as to the assets of the mortgage.

Ownership

Rights to the use, enjoyment, and alienation of property, to the exclusion of others. Concerning real property, absolute rights are rare, being restricted by zoning laws, restrictions, liens, etc.

Open interest

The net amount of outstanding open positions, either long or short, in a given futures or options contract.

P

Pass book

A book of recorded transactions in a savings account, issued by banks and building societies in the UK in which a customer's deposits, withdrawals and interest are entered. The book is retained by the customer to give an indication of the running balance.

Partial Release

Partial Release is a mortgage provision allowing some of the pledged collateral to be released if certain requirements are met.

PAYE (Pay as your earn)

People who earn income from employment or who receive a pension are liable for income tax under the PAYE system.

Taxable pay (gross salary less pension contributions less allowances) is used by the employer to calculate a person's income tax (according to his/her notice of coding) which is passed to the

Inland Revenue usually monthly or weekly. This ensures that employees pay their income tax on a regular basis.

Payment Cap

A Payment Cap is the maximum amount for a payment under an Adjustable Mortgage Loan, regardless of the increase in the interest rate. If the payment is less than the interest alone, negative amortization is created.

Pension Mortgage

A personal mortgage is a type of personal pension plan which utilises the tax free lump sum entitlement from the pension fund at retirement age to repay a mortgage whilst the remainder is used to provide a pension. Throughout the mortgage term the borrower pays interest to the lender such as a building society or bank whilst additionally making payments into the pension scheme. Tax relief is allowable on both the interest payments to the lender and on the contributions to the pension scheme which makes this type of plan attractive.

Personal allowance

Tax allowances are concessions by the Inland Revenue which can be used to reduce a person's Taxable Income. The main allowance for UK taxpayers is the 'personal allowance'; which is an amount of income that is tax free. In the tax year 2005-2006 the personal allowances are:

Under 65: £4,895

65–74: £7,090

75+: £7,220

The personal allowances for elderly people are reduced if their total income exceeds £19,500, and the amount of the reduction if £1 for every £2 of the excess. So someone aged 68 with a Total Income of £19,800 would get a personal allowance of £7,090 less £300 = £6,790.

Personal Equity plan

A plan where people over the age of 18 could formerly invest in the shares of UK and other EC companies via an approved plan manager or through qualifying unit trusts and investment trusts and receive both income and capital gains free of tax.

Personal Income

Personal income is a person's total income which includes salary, transfer payments, dividend and interest income.

Personal Loan

Loans available from banks and other financial institutions to private individuals for personal use such as the purchase of a motor vehicle, holiday or similar item are personal loans. Repayment periods vary from one year to five years. No collateral is asked for or given for the loan.

Personal possessions

The personal possessions of a deceased person which pass to the beneficiary or beneficiaries of the residue of estate unless otherwise stated in the will.

Postal Account

In the UK, a personal account is a building society account in which all transactions are conducted via post. In some cases a pass book is used to record deposits and withdrawals although societies are increasingly acknowledging each of their customer's transactions with a single statement sheet which depicts the amount deposited or withdrawn and the resulting account balance

Pound cost average

In the UK, the regular investing of fixed amounts over regular periods, typically monthly, in order to accumulate holdings in securities such as shares, unit trusts and investment trusts.

When for example a unit trust price or investment trust price has fallen more units or shares can be purchased for that month. Similarly when the price rises then fewer units or shares can be purchased.

Over a period of a few years, the average price paid will be lower than the average share price for that period since more shares are bought at the lower price and fewer at the higher price.

Power of attorney

A document which authorises a person to act on behalf of another is a power of attorney.

Privatization

The sale of government-owned equity in nationalised industries or other commercial enterprises to private investors is the act of privatization.

Property Tax

Local tax assessed on property owned, such as real estate or automobiles.

Public Sector Net Cash Requirement

Formerly known as Public Sector Borrowing Requirement (PSBR), PSNCR is the difference between the expenditure of the public sector and its income.

Where there is a deficit it is financed by borrowing – principally via the sale of government gilt edged stocks (gilts).

Public sector net borrowing also measures the difference between the expenditure and income of the public sector but differs from the net cash requirement in that it is measured on an accruals basis whereas the net cash requirement is mainly a cash measure.

Q

Quick assets

Cash and other assets which can or will be converted into cash fairly soon, such as accounts receivable and marketable securities; or equivalently, current assets minus inventory.

R

Real Asset

An asset that is valuable because of its utility, such as real estate or physical equipment.

Receiver

A person appointed by a court to finalize the affairs of a company and to utilise assets to pay its creditors

Re-mortgage

To re-mortgage is arranging alternative finance for the purchase of a property which is already mortgaged.

Repayment Mortgages

A mortgage where throughout the term, regular payments are made to partly repay interest on the capital and to partly repay the capital itself (the amount of the loan).

Initially the largest proportion of the repayments will be used to pay interest since the capital amount outstanding is at its highest value. Therefore over the initial years the capital will not reduce very much. However as the years proceed more and more of the monthly repayments will be applied to reducing the capital until towards the end of the term the large proportion will be paying off capital and a small proportion paying interest.

Revenue Account

An investment trust term referring to analysis of investment income.

Reverse Mortgage

An arrangement in which a homeowner borrows against the equity in his/her home and receives regular monthly tax-free payments from the lender.

Rollover mortgage

Mortgage for which the unpaid balance is refinanced every few years at then-current rates is a rollover mortgage. This is good for the borrower and bad for the lender if interest rates are falling, and bad for the borrower and good for the lender if interest rates are rising.

S

Salary

Wages received on a regular basis, usually weekly or monthly. Sometimes the term is used to include other benefits, including insurance and a retirement plan.

Savings account

An account with a bank or financial institution which pays interest on balances held, usually once or twice per year, the amount of interest paid usually depends on to the amount of money in the account and the 'base rate' of the Bank of England. There is often a notice period required for withdrawals and in most cases the longer the notice period, the higher the interest rate.

Second Mortgage

A second mortgage is taking out a mortgage on a property which is already mortgaged. This can be used to raise capital if the property has significantly increased in value and would involve finance companies rather than banks or building societies. Since the first mortgagee (lender) usually holds the deeds of the property, the second mortgagee will carry a higher risk and thus charges a considerably higher rate of interest.

Secured Bond

A bond which is secured by the guarantee of assets or collateral is a secured bond.

Secured loan

A loan which is backed up by assets belonging to the borrower (normally property) in order to decrease the risk taken on by the lender. Mortgages and some personal loans are secured loans. If you don't maintain your repayments, your property can be at risk of repossession.

Self assessment

From April 1996 all taxpayers in the UK are obliged by law to maintain records of their income and all types and capital gains so as to enable annual tax returns to be completed. This is known as Self Assessment. In April each year the Inland Revenue sends out almost nine million self assessment forms to taxpayers.

Sequestration

The Scottish legal term for personal bankruptcy is sequestration. This is where an individual, sole trader or partnership is formally declared bankrupt by the court (ie they cannot pay their debts) and that the debts and assets of a person should transfer to an appointed trustee.

Sole trader

An individual proprietor of the simplest form of business, e.g. a shop owned and run by a single person.

Standing order

An instruction you give to your bank or building society to make regular payments from your account to a specific company. This is a fixed amount unlike a direct debit which can vary.

Surplus income

This means the amount of money which you have left over when you subtract necessary expenditure from your income.

T

Tax credits

Tax you receive back in certain circumstances, e.g. pension credit, child tax credit and working tax credit.

Tax Codes

Under the PAYE system of taxing income, tax codes are allocated annually to employees. These codes enable the employer to deduct tax at the correct rate from salaries or wages on a monthly (or weekly) basis for remittance to the Inland Revenue. Most codes show a number followed by a letter. The number refers to the amount of salary payable free of tax (for example if a person's code is 45OH, the tax free allowance will be between £4,500 and £4,509 that is, the first three numbers of the net allowances form the number of the code).

The letter denotes that various personal and other allowances are included.

Taxable earnings

The amount of an individual's annual income on which tax is payable defined as: Taxable earnings = Income - Reliefs - Allowances.

Third Party

A third party is the person who claims against an insured person when loss or damage to property or injury has occurred as a result of the insured person's negligence.

Trustee

A trustee is the person who claims against an insured person when loss or damage to property or injury has occurred as a result of the insured person's negligence.

Trust deed

A form of debt relief where you're unable to pay your debts but have money tied up in assets, such as a house. Creditors can agree that you give everything you own to a trustee (usually an accountant) and sign a trust deed, which is legally binding. The trustee offers to pay your creditors as much as possible of what you owe them from the value of your assets. If it is a protected trust deed then the trust deed is a diligence stopper.

Trustee in bankruptcy

One appointed by a bankruptcy court, and in whom the property of the bankrupt vests. The trustee holds the property in trust, not for the bankrupt, but for the creditors.

Trustor

The borrower under a deed of trust is a trustor.

Trustee

Usually an accountant (a qualified insolvency practitioner), a trustee acts for the creditors by managing the trust deed when a debtor agrees to sign over their assets into a trust deed or when they are declared bankrupt.

U

Unsecured creditor

A creditor who does not hold security (such as a mortgage) for money owed.

Unsecured Loan

An unsecured loan is a loan where the lender has no entitlement to any of the borrower's assets in the event of the borrower failing to make the loan repayments. Such a loan normally carries a higher interest rate than a secured loan.

V

Value

The worth or desirability of something expressed as an amount of money.

Variable interest rate

Interest rates offered by banks and financial institutions on loans or deposits which are liable to change according to circumstances. For example a movement in the interest rate set by the government would usually be an influence.

W

Wrap around mortgage

A second or junior mortgage with a face value of both the amount it secures and the balance due under the first mortgage. The mortgagee under the wrap-around collects a payment based on its face value and then pays the first mortgagee. It is most effective when the first has a lower interest rate than the second, since the mortgagee under the wrap-around gains the difference between the interest rates, or the mortgagor under the wrap-around may obtain a lower rate then if refinancing.